Prayers
in Dialogue

Prayers in Dialogue

For use with Common and Lutheran Lectionaries

Series A

C. David Godshall

C.S.S. Worship Resources Library

PRAYERS IN DIALOGUE

6842 / ISBN 0-89536-813-7   PRINTED IN U.S.A.

INTRODUCTION

This collection of prayers is part of a three-year cycle of prayers for congregational use, related to the three-year lectionary used in many churches. Each prayer attempts to pick up at least one theme of the day, usually from the Gospel reading. Although the first or A year of the series, this is the final one of the three to be written.

By using the voices of pastor, worship assistant, and people in the prayers, an attempt is made to include all who are at worship in the prayer of the church. The whole effort came about in response to comments about the difficulty of staying with a long pastoral prayer. A number of congregations have found the use of *Prayers in Dialogue* a meaningful form of congregational prayer, or an alternative used along with other forms.

For situations in which a worship assistant is not regularly used, a person in the choir, or someone who comes forward from the congregation could read the assistant part. It is also possible for the pastor to do both leadership parts, or one could be assigned to the whole choir or to a section of the congregation. The object is to include many voices in the prayer, and especially to include all the worshiping people in praying.

These prayers are offered to you in the hope of encouraging the people of God to more meaningful prayer in worship, as they are offered to the glory of God, who hears the prayers of all!

C. David Godshall

Dedicated to some significant people in my life,
Luther and Elizabeth Godshall, my late parents
Joseph and Florence Groller, my late parents-in-law

PRAYERS FOR THE LIGHTING OF
THE ADVENT WREATH

The Advent Wreath is a beautiful symbol of preparation during the season when we ready ourselves — spiritually and in other ways — to celebrate the birth of Christ. Many congregations include the lighting of the wreath during Sunday worship the four weeks of Advent. One meaningful way to do this is to identify groups of persons — a traditional family, a group of friends, or persons representative of congregational groups — and have these people participate in the wreath lighting.

Plan ahead: this will help you, as worship leader, and also the persons you will be asking to take part. Include children when they are part of the participating group. Groups can be sisters and brothers, widows/widowers or divorced persons who are friends, and single persons also. The possibilities for groups should be limited only by the make-up of your people.

During worship have the group come forward, with one person designated to read the Scripture that would be appropriate for the wreath lighting. The accompanying prayers are based on the first lesson, taken from the Old Testament. Another in the group can do the actual lighting of the wreath candle. If the wreath is near the altar or communion table on which there are lighted candles, have a taper or candlelighter available; or, the acolyte could either bring a lighted taper to the person who will do the lighting, or do the lighting her/himself.

All in the group can then lead in the prayer. Five voices are designated, one usually appropriate for a younger person. If there are less in the group, persons would read more than one part.

Following the prayer, as those in the group return to their places in the church, the congregation could sing a verse of a familiar hymn for Advent.

ADVENT 1 — *Theme:* Peace
Suggested reading: Isaiah 2:1-5

Prayer:

Voice 1: Bring peace to our world and to our lives, Lord God, as you call people to faith in the One who walked in your light.

Voice 2: You give us peace with you through our Savior, Jesus Christ, who takes away the sin which separates us from you, O God.

Voice 3: You make people long for peace and cry out for a day when war and strife will be no more.

Voice 4: You give us the vision of standing in your presence, at peace with all those around us, and at peace with you, our God.

Voice 5: We pray for your peace, O God.

All: Amen.

ADVENT 2 — *Theme:* Harmony
Suggested reading: Isaiah 11:1-10

Prayer:

Voice 1: The discord of peoples, of nature, and of powers weighs heavily upon us, O God.

Voice 2: Grant us leaders of wisdom, those who will rule with justice and integrity.

Voice 3: Inspire all peoples to a reverence of you, Lord God.

Voice 4: Make your Son the symbol of righteousness for all nations, and send your people to share his Good News with everyone.

Voice 5: We pray for harmony with you, and with one another, O God.

All: Amen.

ADVENT 3 — *Theme:* Joy
Suggested reading: Isaiah 35:1-10

Prayer:
Voice 1: Lift us to the thrill of beauty in your world, O God; for all that you have made is good.
Voice 2: Lift us to the vitality of new strength, O God, that we may take hold of the tasks you invite us to do.
Voice 3: Lift us with miracles of handicaps overcome, of wholeness restored to your people and to your world, O God.
Voice 4: Lift us to the highway on which your people make their way into your presence, O God.
Voice 5: We pray for joy with you, O God.
All: Amen.

ADVENT 4 — *Theme:* A Sign
Suggested reading: Isaiah 7:10-17
Prayer:
Voice 1: Draw our attention from all the claims and promises which confuse us, Lord.
Voice 2: Keep us from refusing your invitation to seek your help and grace.
Voice 3: Open our eyes to the sign you set before us — the babe in a manger, the boy about his Father's business, the man in ministry, the innocent one on the cross, the victor over sin and death!
Voice 4: You have come among us, Lord, and you are with us always.
Voice 5: We pray for you, Jesus, to be our Lord.
All: Amen.

Advent 1

Pastor: We know the darkness of this world, O God; for we have groped about in darkness and despaired of ever finding light.

Assistant: Our own sin can overwhelm us,

People: And make it impossible for us to find good in anything.

Assistant: The evil around us can be overpowering,

People: And make us too frightened to reach out with efforts of good.

Assistant: The onslaughts of the Evil One can crush our faith,

People: And make us give up even our trust in you, O God.

Pastor: Help us to look to the horizon, to see the coming day, to find the light which is come into the world, to hope for victory over darkness and for the brilliance of righteousness.

Assistant: A new day has dawned for each of us;

People: For in baptism, we have been made the children of God.

Assistant: The evil in our world must contend with people of good will;

People: For we who trust in God reach out to one another and to those in need of love, hope, and freedom from fear.

Assistant: The Evil One is not in control;

People: For our Lord Jesus Christ has been victorious over sin and death, and lives to come again in power and might.

Pastor: Turn us to your light, O God. Give us strength to strive for good, to bring about a new start for ourselves and others, to use all of the gracious help you give us to live as those who walk in light.

Assistant: Forgive our sin, Lord God,

People: That we may stand in your presence and receive your powerful love into our lives.

Assistant: Use your people to strive against the world's evil,

People: Arming us with the weapons of peace, joy, hope, and love.

Assistant: Destroy the Evil One for all eternity,

People: As you make all things new and fulfill the victory Christ won for us on the cross of Calvary.

(Other petitions may be included here.)

Pastor: You are coming to us, Lord Jesus; we would be ready to stand in your presence. So, by the Spirit's power, help us to leave the ways of sin and use the weapons and tools you graciously give to conquer evil and darkness.

All: So may we stand in your light now and forever. *Amen (Our Father . . .)*

Advent 2

Pastor: Almighty God, you consistently guide and help those who turn to you; and, even when we stray and ignore you, you reach out to correct and restore us.

Assistant: You judge us with fairness,

People: Providing us with many insights into life.

Assistant: You punish evil,

People: So that we learn the failure of wrong ways of living.

Assistant: You teach the way of righteousness,

People: Showing us the power of love to overcome evil, and giving us the example of many who have responded to your love.

Pastor: Heavenly Lord, you have started us on the way of salvation by turning us from sin and its power to defeat and destroy.

Assistant: Voices like those of John the Baptist have warnea us;

People: And, in our need, we turn to hear the warning voices and repent.

Assistant: Leaders have set forth wisdom;

People: And we have wanted to grow and learn to respond to you.

Assistant: Jesus Christ has fulfilled promises given;

People: And, in him, our salvation has been worked out. Help us to follow where Christ has led the way!

Pastor: Help us to live as your people, O God, dwelling with us as powerful Spirit. Give us all that we need to be the voices, leaders, and followers of Christ for our time.

Assistant: Send us the Spirit, and put the fire of his working into us,

People: That we may receive, and pass on to all we meet, the blessings of joy, peace, hope, and love.

(Other petitions may be included here.)

Pastor: We, your children, pray that we may lead all the world to find you, O God.

All: And help everyone to know the joy of salvation through Jesus Christ. *Amen (Our Father . . .)*

Advent 3

Pastor: We, your people, are waiting, O God — waiting for your promises to be fulfilled; waiting for the last day on which all things will be made new; waiting for ourselves to be saved and brought into your perfect presence.

Assistant: Your people have often waited, Lord.

People: Prophets of long ago spoke your word, and awaited your actions.

Assistant: Your people have questioned their waiting, Lord.

People: John sent messengers to ask Jesus if he was the expected one.

Assistant: We are waiting, Lord.

People: At times we become impatient, weary, concerned that our waiting may never end.

Pastor: You have given us glimpses of what you will do, and examples of what you will bring to pass, Lord God.

Assistant: A desert lies bare and dry.

People: But when you send rain upon it, it flowers with incredible beauty.

Assistant: A highway stretches to the horizon.

People: But when your people follow it, it brings them to your presence, rejoicing.

Assistant: Marvelous reversals happen:

People: The blind see, the deaf hear, the lame walk, the dumb speak, the dead live, and those in need hear good news.

Pastor: Help us, O God, to await your holy day patiently — with hope in what we know you will do; with trust that we will be part of your new creation; with joy that our salvation has already begun.

Assistant: Help us to live together in love,

People: Caring for one another as we recognize our Lord in each one we meet.

Assistant: Help us to be about your work —

People: Spreading good news, speaking truth, sharing what we are given, remaining your faithful people.

Assistant: Help us to stand with you at the last,

People: Sharing the full joy of your presence with all around us, and with all who have trusted in you in their time.

(Other petitions may be included here.)

Pastor: We await your coming, Lord — to us, day by day; to your world to make it new; to the new kingdom you have promised.

All: Come, Lord Jesus! *Amen (Our Father . . .)*

Advent 4

Pastor: We find your way of coming to us and of working with us unusual, Lord God. Our world teaches us to expect something different, or to expect nothing at all.

Assistant: We have developed a liking for the sensational.

People: But you come to us quietly, in simplicity, with gentleness and sincerity.

Assisant: We bow to power and to wealth.

People: But you ask us to kneel in awe at a manger, with shepherds and young parents and stable animals.

Assisant: We hear the whisper that you are not real, that you do not exist.

People: But you have met people in ages past, and you continue to find a place in the hearts of people today.

Pastor: We never cease to find wonder and awe when we consider your ways, O Lord. No matter how many times we have reviewed your actions, they bring us meaning and possibility all over again as we live them now.

Assistant: You are born among us, Lord Jesus:

People: Born to a maiden, part of the family of David, known to us as the very Son of God.

Assistant: You fulfill the promise of old, Lord Jesus,

People: Yet you make your own way, stand forth as an unexpected Messiah, win our salvation in victory over a terrible death.

Assistant: You are Immanuel:

People: God with us — present now and forever.

Pastor: Everyone who follows you, Jesus, is a miracle of the faith worked in us by the Holy Spirit. We cannot explain your love. We cannot force true faith from others. We can but live your love and invite others to believe in you.

Assistant: You have made us your disciples;

People: And we pray you to keep us in the company of your people throughout our lives, and in the life to come.

(Other petitions may be included here.)

Pastor: Glory and praise and honor unto you, O God, for you have come to save us, your people, and you now live and reign to all eternity — one God, holy and mighty, yet merciful and gracious to all who know you.

All: May we know you forever, O God. *Amen (Our Father . . .)*

Family Prayer for Christmas

Assistant: Over many centuries, people have believed in you, O God, and have celebrated the night of Jesus' birth. Help us to be conscious this night of those first believers who were called to follow Jesus.

Pastor: Thank you for the first to be aware of Jesus' coming:

People: For shepherds and stable helpers and townsfolk who saw the newborn Christ Child, and heard his infant cry.

Pastor: Thank you for the first disciples and followers of your Son:

People: For Peter and John, for Martha and Salome, for unnamed persons whose lives were made new as they heard his voice and answered his call.

Pastor: Thank you for those who established the church, and set the Good News into written form:

People: For Mark and Matthew, Luke and John, for people who lent their homes and used their gifts to encourage the fellowship of your people.

Assistant: Year upon year your living Word was not lost, but was shown forth to generation after generation of your people.

Pastor: Thank you for leaders such as Justin, Augustine, and Gregory,

People: And for their carrying the church through ages both dark and golden.

Family Prayer for Christmas

Pastor: Thank you for reformers such as John Hus, Martin Luther, and John Calvin,

People: Who thought through the Good News for their own time, and called your people to renewal.

Pastor: Thank you for persons like Albert Schweitzer, Martin Luther King, Jr., and Father Jerzy Popieluszko* (YEH-zhe Pohp-yeh-WOOSH-koh),

People: And for their sacrifices in seeking to serve their sisters and brothers in Christ.

Assistant: Many of us are aware of those of our own families who have worshiped before you, often helping us to discover the faith we call our own.

Pastor: Thank you for grandparents, parents, and relatives who have been part of your church —

People: For the models they provided us, and for the challenges they gave us to reach beyond their own experiences.

Pastor: Thank you for our family in the faith, those among whom we study and worship and serve,

People: For the support and encouragement and challenge that grows out of our shared life in Christ.

Assistant: In all of our remembering of others, let us recommit ourselves to faith and trust in the One you have given us:

All: Jesus the Christ, our Savior, in whom we see your love, O God, and through whom we are given eternal life. *Amen (Our Father . . .)*

Father Jerzy Popieluszko was a Polish priest murdered in 1984 for his support of Solidarity.

Christmas Eve

Pastor: In awe we come to you in prayer, Lord God, for we are here to celebrate your coming among us in a most wonderful manner, in the birth of Jesus, your Son, our Lord.

Assistant: A child is born; a Son is given,

People: To share with us all that life means, all that life holds, and to show us life in relationship to you, our God.

Assistant: This child will rule over us,

People: Not as an earthly king with might and force; but, in the power of your love, he will rule us righteously.

Pastor: For ages, your people have delighted in your presence in Jesus of Nazareth, and have called him by the names your prophet wrote.

Assistant: Jesus is the Wonderful Counselor,

People: The Mighty God in our midst.

Assistant: He and the Everlasting Father are one.

People: He is the Prince of Peace, taking away the enmity between God and his people.

Pastor: Lord God, you have done this marvelous action for us; help us to ponder all that it means for us.

Assistant: Help us to give up all that is ungodly.

People: By your grace, turn us from sin.

Assistant: Help us to anticipate the day of your coming ful-fillment,

People: Living now under your control, in lives that reflect your goodness.

(Other petitions may be included here.)

Pastor: May we go forth from our worship this night rejoic-ing in all you have done for us,

People: And live our lives as a praise to you, the Lord our God.

All: *Amen (Our Father . . .)*

Christmas Day

Pastor: Lord God, you have sent many messengers to your people.

Assistant: How wonderful to see those who share Good News with us;

People: Yet, after hearing them, your people have often turned from the messengers, and gone their own way.

Pastor: Lord God, you have done many good things for your people.

Assistant: How generous you are with your blessings and your grace;

People: Yet, after receiving them, your people have often forgotten you, and have gloried in their own efforts.

Pastor: Lord God, you have called people to come to you in faith.

Assistant: How merciful you have been to allow us to be in your presence;

People: Yet, after knowing you, your people have often rejected you, and have given their loyalties to other things.

Pastor: Then you sent a new messenger unto us:

Assistant: Even Christ, our Lord.

People: That, in him, we might see the height and depth, the length and breadth of your love for us.

Pastor: Standing among us was the one who created all things,

Assistant: And who gave up that power to experience our life here.

People: That, in him, we might know grace and truth.

Pastor: Our friend, Jesus, gave himself for us

Assistant: And won victory over sin and death,

People: That he would be our Lord and Savior.

Pastor: Your Word, O God, is in our world now.

Assistant: He is your living Son, raised from death, with you for all eternity;

People: And with us, your people, that we can believe through him, be saved from all that would separate us from you, and receive your gift of eternal life with him.

Pastor: We welcome you to our lives, O God.

Assistant: Come to us and dwell with us,

People: This day and every day, keeping us members of your kingdom now and forever.

All: *Amen (Our Father . . .)*

Christmas 1

Pastor: Lord God, it has often been your will to call your people through the promises of your servants, assuring us that you desire our good, that you are committed to our well-being.

Assistant: Centuries ago you had your prophet speak of your unfailing love;

People: He reminded the people of all that God had done because of his mercy and love.

Assistant: But the best news that he shared was of the coming of one who would save the people.

People: The savior would be God himself, the God who had always taken care of his own.

Pastor: All of us recognize, O God, the special time in which you fulfilled your promise.

Assistant: Calling a human mother to trust you, you entered our realm as one of us.

People: You lived under the law given to guide your people, to show them their need of you.

Assistant: Calling a faithful human father to accept this special child as his own, you protected him from human hatred.

People: Your Word came true as your special servant came out of Egypt, and was a Nazarene.

Pastor: In our own time, Lord God Almighty, you continue to reveal yourself and the special ways in which we are blessed because of the coming of your Son.

Assistant: Christ Jesus fulfilled the law for us.

People: And though we are sinners, Jesus calls us into fellowship with you through the forgiveness of our sins.

Assistant: Jesus your Son has made us brothers and sisters, children of the holy parent of all peoples,

People: So that, by your Spirit, we can call to you, "Father, my Father," and know ourselves to be your children.

(Other petitions may be included here.)

Pastor: Fulfill your promise for each of us this day, Lord God.

Assistant: Redeem us and make us your sons and daughters.

People: Free us from slavery to sin and stand us within your kingdom.

All: To you be all praise and thanksgiving for sending us your Son! *Amen (Our Father . . .)*

Name of Jesus — New Year's Day

Assistant: Through many ages, the newborn have held a special place in the minds and hearts of your people, O God.

People: We rejoice with one another at each new birth, asking parents the name of their child.

Pastor: At creation, you gave to the man the delightful task of naming every creature, and, by the names given, each creature was known. Even today our relationships with one another are enabled by the names we are given, the names which speak of who we are.

Assistant: In our rebellion and sin, we, at times, make of names mere labels with which to shout or curse those for whom hatred wells up in our hearts.

People: Even your name, O God, is carelessly spoken, cruelly misused, dangerously uttered in oaths of anger.

Pastor: Help us to recognize the meaning in each and every name, the ways in which we touch and affect persons as we speak their names, and the responsibility we have for caring for those whose names are known to us.

Assistant: This is a day of new beginnings, Lord. Make it a time of renewal as your people gathered here lay before you the good and bad of a year past, and set forth on the adventure of the future.

People: You know us, O God; our names are before you and our hearts are open to you.

Name of Jesus — New Year's Day

Pastor: May we rejoice in this closeness to you which gives us status as your children. Work in us the completeness of your salvation, and put in us the will to serve you as we live.

All: As you have brought us to this day, so keep us in the days ahead, and hold us unto you that we may be named those who will stand in your presence eternally. *Amen (Our Father . . .)*

Christmas 2

Assistant: We your people rejoice in all that you have done for us, O God.

Pastor: You have saved your people

People: When you came to us in Jesus.

Pastor: You have made losers into victors

People: When you overthrew sin and won clear victory with love.

Pastor: You have given us a new name,

People: That by our discipleship to the Christ we may be known forever.

Assistant: We thank you, God, for the gracious love which was intended for us from the very beginning of creation.

Pastor: We have not chosen you, Lord, but you have called us to faith:

People: Announcing good news of sins forgiven, of grace freely bestowed.

Pastor: We could not work our way to you, Lord, but you have given us your Spirit:

People: Empowering us to pray, to trust, to hope, to rejoice.

Pastor: Even now we are unsure of being able to please you;

People: But Christ stands before us, and in him we are welcomed into your holy presence.

Assistant: We ask you, God, to come to us and live in us, that we may be your people, faithful servants of the truth and light which transforms this dark world.

Pastor: You send your called people into the world,

People: That we may share a message of hope to all we meet.

Pastor: You do not separate us from needs and hurts and pains,

People: That we may bring your healing, helping, and saving to those who need it most.

Pastor: We are sometimes almost engulfed by the thorough darkness of the world around us.

People: Yet, you will not allow the light that you have given people of faith to be extinguished.

(Other petitions may be included here.)

Assistant: Continue to make us your people, to bless us as we trust in you, to send us out in your name as your presence to others.

All: And go with us, Lord God, for only as you *do* can we live for you and come to your eternal kingdom. *Amen (Our Father . . .)*

Epiphany

Pastor: We pray, Lord God, for nations and peoples this day; you have made us all, and you desire that all of us come to you to know the peace of your grace and love.

Assistant: There is much darkness in our world, God.

People: People are turned away from you, lost in sin, crushed under burdens of guilt, oppression, and ignorance.

Assistant: Even those who name you Lord need light rekindled in them.

People: Your faithful are overwhelmed by evil, appalled by tragedy, and in fear of terror.

Pastor: We look to you for the shining light that overcomes darkness, for the forgiveness which overcomes sin, for the faith and trust which overcomes evil.

People: Grant us these gifts for the sake of your Son, our Lord.

Pastor: We pray, Lord God, for all sorts and conditions of people this day; you know us all, and you desire that all will live in the glory of your presence.

Assistant: There are many who have not heard of you, God.

People: People turn from you, and do not tell their children of your being God.

Assistant: There are many who reject you, God.

People: In frustration, anger, and just plain rebellion, people refuse to believe, to trust, to recognize your love.

Pastor:　　We believe that you pursue us even in our rebellion, that you try again and again to turn people to you.

People:　　Grant us your constant presence, that we may never turn to you and find ourselves alone.

Pastor:　　We pray, Lord God, for those around us and for those who are yet to come into your world, that through your believing people, they may hear the Good News and respond to you.

Assistant:　Make us salt, leaven, and light, O Lord,

People:　　That we may flavor and permeate and brighten the lives of those we touch.

Assistant:　Move us to reach to all those near us, and to make possible the proclaiming of your Good News to every place on this earth.

People:　　Make us your witnesses, and enable us to strengthen your mission to all, through our prayers and gifts.

Pastor:　　Your secret was revealed to your people as you brought Jews and Gentiles together into your church, that Jesus Christ would be Lord and Savior of all.

People:　　Grant today that all races, classes, nationalities, and cultures will turn to belief in you, O God.

(Other petitions may be included here.)

Pastor:　　We rejoice in your coming among us in Jesus Christ, O God. Keep us through your Holy Spirit, that we may stand with you in your eternal kingdom.

All:　　　Amen (Our Father . . .)

32

The Baptism of Our Lord
First Sunday After the Epiphany

Assistant: How valuable you have made our baptisms, Lord God, for your sinless Son also entered the water to receive the gifts of your promise.

Pastor: John recognized your chosen one, O God, and would have changed places with him.

People: Yet Jesus did not hold himself aloof, but identified with those who responded to John's call for repentance and new life.

Assistant: You made clear your blessing for your Son, appearing to him and declaring him the one with whom you are pleased.

Pastor: What affirmation that announcement brought to your beloved!

People: What confidence it brings to us as we place our faith and trust in Jesus, who is our Savior!

Assistant: The pattern for living which you set forth for us through your Son is a model of love and caring.

Pastor: Jesus did not give up on the weakest or least likely to respond.

People: Those just about broken by sin are his concern; those in whom the light of hope has just about gone out are his mission.

Assistant: And so you establish your covenant with us, Lord God, and make us your people, that we may carry on the life Jesus modeled for us.

The Baptism of Our Lord
First Sunday After the Epiphany

Pastor: You have given us your call to proclaim Good News, to give help, to restore hope.

People: Help us to announce your grace for all, to speak your forgiving word, to reassure those who respond to your presence.

(Other petitions may be included here.)

Assistant: Fill us with your Spirit, and give this gift of power to all who are baptized in your holy name, that we may walk in new life and rejoice in your favor, now and forever.

All: *Amen (Our Father . . .)*

Epiphany 2

Assistant: Thank you, Lord God, for sending your Son to individual persons, who responded to their friend's introduction.

Pastor: John announced to Andrew and his friend, "There is the Lamb of God."

People: May we behold the Lamb of God and go with him, calling others to come and know the annointed one of God.

Assistant: Thank you, Lord God, for gathering congregations of people who respond to your giving them unity in Jesus, the Lord.

Pastor: Paul greeted those who were in fellowship at Corinth, and gave thanks for their partnership in the Gospel.

People: May we rejoice in the fellowship we have with your people in our congregation, and feel the unity we have with all your believing people everywhere.

Assistant: Thank you, Lord God, for appointing your Son as the one who gathers your scattered people, and who stirs faith in peoples of all nations.

Pastor: Renew our commitment to your one, holy, catholic, and apostolic church.

People: Renew in your church that sense of mission which sends us to those near and far with your Good News.

Assistant: Thank you, Lord God, for your presence with each person, and for your uniting us in the fellowship of all believers.

Pastor: Strengthen our witness to your Son, Jesus Christ.

People: Empower our living in righteousness and with compassion.

(Other petitions may be included here.)

Assistant: Bring from your people responsible witness, caring service, and loving worship, that we may show ourselves to be part of your kingdom now, and worthy to stand with you on the day when Christ comes to rule in glory.

All: Amen (Our Father . . .)

Epiphany 3

Pastor: The beginning of your ministry, O Lord Jesus, was done among those who needed most to hear your call. We are thankful in our time for ministries which reach out to those who walk in darkness.

Assistant: Each young person is unaware of you until he or she is taught of your love by parents, teachers, and fellow Christians.

People: Help us to fulfill vows made at baptism to help our children live godly lives until the day you come again.

Assistant: Around us there are those for whom life has little meaning or value, because they have never come to know you as their Savior.

People: Send us to neighbors, co-workers, friends, and all we meet as witnesses to your love, given us on the cross of Calvary.

Assistant: In our world there are those who have not heard the Good News, who live in the shadow of unbelief or false belief.

People: Gather from your people the prayers, the gifts, and the committed persons through whom your message of saving, healing love will be made known to all.

Pastor: As people respond to your Gospel and turn to you in repentance, make them of one mind and heart, so that in our lives of faith we may find true power only in your death for us.

Assistant: Overcome divisions among us which are based on personality, jealousy, or envy.

People: Draw us into the common tasks of praising you, serving others in your name, and presenting a loving witness to all.

Assistant: Even as we appreciate our histories, help us to let go of outdated traditions and biases so that we can discover anew the unity you bring to our faith.

People: For there is one Lord, one faith, one baptism, one God and Father of all people. We praise you alone, Lord Jesus Christ!

Assistant: As we help to bring people of the world to faith in you, allow us to learn from them the excitement and joy of newly found hope.

People: Keep us from burdening them with our past disagreements, and help us to stand side by side with them in our response to all you have done to save us.

(Other petitions may be included here.)

Pastor: Through your church in all the world, Lord Jesus, work the gifts of your spirit, that in our time your Good News may be heard by everyone, and that day arrive in which you shall return in glory to receive all who trust you into eternal peace and joy.

All: Amen. Come, Lord Jesus! *(Our Father . . .)*

Epiphany 4

Pastor: It is so easy for us to get caught up in living the way of those who do not honor you, O God, for they are all around us, and their ways are very persuasive to us.

Assistant: We want others to like us,

People: Instead of being willing to endure persecution.

Assistant: We want to be successful,

People: Instead of being willing to be poor or humble.

Assistant: We want to go our own way, to please ourselves,

People: Instead of being willing to do what you require — showing mercy to others.

Pastor: Forgive us, O God, and call us anew to the path which leads to your kingdom.

All: Hear us, for Jesus' sake.

Pastor: We would like assurances which prove your way for us; that make clear to others we have made the best choice; that leave no room for the doubts which nibble away at our faith.

Assistant: We want some visible way of proving you,

People: Instead of being willing to trust your Word to us.

Assistant: We want some special knowledge of all you will do,

People: Instead of being willing to rely on your promises.

Assistant: We want to be strong through our religious beliefs and practices,

People: Instead of being willing to place our whole confidence in what you have done for us in Christ Jesus.

Pastor: Renew in us a childlike faith which depends solely on you and recognizes your power to save us.

All: Hear us, for Jesus' sake.

Pastor: As we live, we attempt to appease you with special religious actions and practices, thinking we can then conduct ourselves however we please the rest of the time.

Assistant: We want to be as free of you as we wish,

People: Instead of being willing to have you a part of all we do.

Assistant: We want to decide how to respond to those around us,

People: Instead of being willing to use your guidance for our relationships.

Assistant: We want to give you things,

People: Instead of being willing to show justice, love kindness, and walk humbly with you.

Pastor: Help us to recall all of your mighty actions for us, and to realize how you have saved us from destruction, that we may be your faithful, trusting people, alive with your spirit.

All: Hear us, for Jesus' sake.

(Other petitions may be included here.)

Pastor: Make us happy and blessed as we walk in your presence, depend only on you, and reflect your love to all around us — by the power of your Spirit, in the ways shown us by Jesus our Savior, to the glory of your most holy name.

All: *Amen (Our Father . . .)*

Epiphany 5

Pastor: Lord God, you have given us commands, and you have called us to a way of life which shows discipline and restraint. Help us to comprehend that your call is not a restriction on our living, but, rather, enables us to be responsible, caring, loving persons.

Assistant: Help us not to chafe at doing what is good,

People: But to experience that moral living is good for us, and good for those around us.

Assistant: Help us not to use religion to hurt and punish ourselves,

People: But to work out of our beliefs as we effectively help to conquer some of the ills of our world.

Pastor: Lord God, you have invited us to be your people, not by using our cleverness, but by trusting in your resounding action for us in the death and resurrection of Jesus Christ. Help us to use the power of his life as we live our lives in response to you.

Assistant: Help us to flavor the families, the neighborhoods, the groups in which we live,

People: With the words we speak, the deeds we do, the attitudes we reveal, and the goals we seek to accomplish.

Assistant: Help us to light up the relationships, the responsibilities, the opportunities we have daily,

People: With the way we care, the way we listen, the way we smile, the way we forgive, and the way we get involved.

Pastor: Lord God, at your bidding, people through many ages have developed ways to express their devotion to you. Help us to use worship, prayer, fasting, and the giving of gifts in positive, effective ways which will further your kingdom.

Assistant: May we not turn these religious practices into selfish exercises of pride,

People: But make them the basis on which we work to improve the lives of those around us.

Assistant: May we not allow these religious practices to be words only, devoid of actions and deeds which show them to be genuine,

People: But make them the foundation on which we build communities of integrity, caring, helping, and sharing.

(Other petitions may be included here.)

Pastor: Lord God, we ask your help in living out the deeds of those who are the followers of your Son. Strengthen our trust that you will bring healing, salvation, protection, and answer to our prayers as we do.

All: Through Jesus Christ our Lord. *Amen (Our Father . . .)*

Epiphany 6

Assistant: How can we measure up to what you announce, Lord Jesus? Here we are, trying to be fairly good people, and you declare that unless we are pure of heart, we have condemned ourselves!

Pastor: Few of us have raised our hand to take the life of another,

People: But who of us has not been angry with another, or harbored hatred against another in our hearts?

Pastor: Few of us have permitted our lust to get us wrongly involved with another person,

People: But who of us has not had lust stir in our thoughts?

All: We beseech you to hear our honest cry, as we admit that we don't live up to your demands, O Lord. Forgive us.

Assistant: You describe the kind of behavior which betrays faithfulness to God, Lord Jesus. Yet, here we are, aware that we give in to such ways of trying to resolve the tensions of living.

Pastor: We cut some corners, try to take advantage of situations, or rush into deals without thinking them through;

People: And, should another sue us to resolve the results of our less than honorable actions, we seek out a clever lawyer rather than working out a fair solution.

Pastor: We may be unable to curb our desires, and we do not always try our hardest to work out our relationships;

People: And, should our desire lead us into sin, we have no intention of gouging an eye or dismembering a limb for what *everyone does*. Or should a relationship break down, we quickly want to be done with it and get on with living.

Pastor:	We are part of a society in which very few people trust others, because we have become used to saying almost anything without really meaning to follow through on our words.
People:	Therefore, we attempt to convince others we are sincere by swearing on all that's holy and all that's unholy as well, and no one expects just a *yes* or *no*.
All:	We simply do not listen to your insights for living, Lord Jesus. Forgive us.
Assistant:	It sounds harsh when we read your commands to your people of long ago, asking them to choose between life and death. Yet we pray you to help us see that you would give us life, and want only that we would accept your way, which shows that life is what we choose.
Pastor:	You showed us that to obey the commandments and laws of our God is not the requirement for salvation.
People:	Salvation is your gift to us, Lord Jesus Christ, our Savior!
Pastor:	You have taught us that our obedience, our taking to heart your wisdom for living, our finding truth in your picture of life are actions of acceptance.
People:	Living your way means we accept your gift, value your love, and rejoice in your blessings.
All:	We need your help this day and every day so that we may choose life!

(Other petitions may be included here.)

Pastor:	O Almighty God, our creator and redeemer and sanctifier, fill us with your power, without which we cannot come to faith, and go with us day by day so that we may humbly and respectfully respond to you in everything that we say and do.
All:	In Jesus' name we pray. *Amen (Our Father . . .)*

Epiphany 7

Assistant: One of the ways in which we understand that we are your people, O God, is to picture ourselves as builders.

People: We are builders of faith in Jesus Christ our Lord.

Pastor: Guide us, O God, to have Christ as the one and only foundation of our faith, and to build upon that foundation trust and confidence which will see us through all of the changes and chances of this life.

People: We are builders of communities of faith, in which ministry is done in your name.

Pastor: Call us to the fellowship of your church, O God, that we may bring together our many abilities, be encouraged through our working together, and develop a congregation in which actions of kindness and caring take place.

Assistant: You have announced to us that we are your temples, O God, the places in which you dwell, the places in which we meet you and have relationship with you.

People: Help us not to destroy this place of your dwelling by our unfaithfulness, or by our neglect of those things which produce vital life.

Pastor: We are your creation, O God, and into us you have breathed your spirit. Give us such a sense of being yours that we will rejoice in our blessings, and respond to you with faithfulness and love.

Assistant: It is your desire to give us all that we need, O God, and to provide us with all that we should know in order to be yours now and eternally.

People: Still, we are tempted to listen to the wisdom of the world, which leads us at times to reject your ways and to try those which unbelieving humans have devised.

Pastor: Defend us against this wile of the Devil, and show us again and again the foolishness of living by any other way than yours.

People: Help us when we attempt to replace your wisdom with our own, and strengthen us when we discover that all things are ours through Christ our Lord.

Pastor: Bless us with the presence of Jesus in our lives, helping us to affirm him our Lord, helping us to follow his way, and helping us to witness his power to save.

(Other petitions may be included here.)

Assistant: You alone are God, and to you alone we owe our lives and our allegiance. Renew in us the faith which will hold us to you in hope until that day when we stand in your presence for all eternity.

All: Amen (Our Father . . .)

Epiphany 8

Pastor: Through the example of our Lord Jesus, and through the teaching of the Apostle Paul, we know ourselves to be servants in your name, O Lord.

Assistant: You, O God, require one thing of your servants:

People: That we be faithful to you, our master.

Assistant: Help us to be servants for the sake of the Gospel,

People: Willing and ready to share the Good News with others, and to serve the needs of others in your name.

Pastor: Many judgments are made of your people, O Lord, by those who live and work with us in the church, and by those who stand outside your church.

Assistant: You ask us not to pass judgment on one another, and you declare that the judgments of others are not to be our guide.

People: You alone are the one who can judge, O God, for you alone can see what is deep in the minds and hearts of those you have made.

Assistant: Judge us in righteousness, O Lord:

People: And forgive our sins that we may live.

Pastor: Our lives in this world sometimes become confused in unfair comparisons, being taken for granted, and being exploited.

Assistant: Jesus has announced that we are blessed when we are persecuted for your sake.

People: Help us to be willing to accept the false judgments of this world, and to receive the blessings of your love.

Assistant: Others, at times, gain fame and fortune, while it seems that we do the work and see through the problems of life.

People: Help us to be willing to overlook inequities, and to entrust ourselves to the rewards that you promise to your faithful ones.

(Other petitions may be included here.)

Pastor: You show us, O God, that life in this world is affected by sin, and cannot be what you intended it to be; so help us to trust you now, through trials and temptations, that we may rejoice in your holy and loving presence forever.

All: Through Jesus Christ our Lord. *Amen (Our Father . . .)*

Transfiguration of Our Lord

Pastor: We praise and glorify you, O God, that you have come to us and revealed to us your holiness, righteousness, and love.

Assistant: When seeing your glory, people have often fallen down in fear and trembling;

People: But again and again you have declared that we need not fear you, and are to rejoice in your glorious presence.

Assistant: At times we cannot quite fathom the power of your presence;

People: But you implore us to be patient, and to trust that we will understand all things in your good time.

Pastor: Each age of your people longs for its own experiences of your presence. This day we give thanks that you appeared to the disciples and helped them share their experiences in Scripture.

Assistant: We thank you for Peter, and for those who were his fellow workers in establishing the church.

People: Give us their confidence to believe, and keep their word before us as a shining lamp.

Assistant: Give us the vision to see the possibilities of faith for ourselves and for your people today,

People: That we may strive together to be your people, with the help of your Holy Spirit.

The Transfiguration of Our Lord

Pastor: If we are attentive, there is evidence enough of your working in this our time. Make each of us a part of your miracle as we continue in faith despite many obstacles; and make your church the continuous miracle which prevails against the gates of hell.

Assistant: We are aware that many times, and at any time, we could fall away from you, O God.

People: The fact that we believe is a miracle; that we try to live our faith is an evidence of your power; that we persevere in our belief is your marvelous doing.

Assistant: We are conscious that every generation might be the last one to be your church, O God.

People: The fact that corruption, envy, malice, pride, greed, and so many more sins have not destroyed your church is a miracle; that your church lives on, even when divided, is evidence of your love: that your people continue in spite of the derision of the world is your wondrous activity among us.

(Other petitions may be included here.)

Pastor: Continue to show us your glory, Lord God, as you hold before us the vision of your Son, Jesus, who lives and reigns with you in glory, and who will come to us in your good time to bring all who trust you into your perfect kingdom.

All: With the Holy Spirit, and you, O God, Christ is one in power, honor, and might, now and forever. *Amen (Our Father . . .)*

Ash Wednesday

Assistant: Today, O Lord God, you declare to us our mortality; you remind us that we were created of the dust of the earth, and to that dust we shall return.

Pastor: Lord, we glory in our creation, as we stand in awe of your power to bring forth life.

People: Your gift is more than biological life, O God; you desire us to live as in your image.

Pastor: Now, Lord, help us to trust you in the face of death.

People: For although we are mortal, you have given us the promise of resurrection to eternal life.

Assistant: Today, O Lord God, you call us to repentance; you remind us that all have sinned, and none deserve your grace.

Pastor: We earnestly seek your forgiveness and your renewal for our lives.

People: Your gift deals with sin as we could never cope with it; it is your gracious desire to forgive.

Pastor: Now, Lord, help us to seek your forgiveness in the face of judgment and condemnation.

People: For you have assured us of your love in Jesus, the Christ, and we place our trust in him.

Assistant: Today, O Lord God, you lead us forth on the journey of Lent; you remind us it is in welcoming Jesus into our lives that we have hope.

Pastor: Lord, we glory in your having sent Jesus to save us from sin and death.

People: Your gift of a savior is more than we deserve, more than we can imagine.

Pastor: Now, Lord, send your Spirit to us that we may turn to Jesus with sincerity, and receive all he offers us.

People: For with Jesus as our Lord and Savior, we can set aside fear and live with peace in our hearts and love in our actions.

(Other petitions may be included here.)

Pastor: Blessed God, our lives are in your hand. You have made us, and you alone can give us new, eternal life. Hold us in your love today and every day, and help us to respond to all you have done for us with lives given to your service.

All: Through Jesus Christ, your Son, our Lord. *Amen (Our Father . . .)*

Lent 1

Assistant: Lord God, where can we turn when we are tempted? Who will hear us when we groan under the weight of sin? Is there any to see us when we covertly engage in what we know is wrong?

People: You, O God, walk with us day by day, every day, all the time — not to check up on us, but to offer your saving help when we turn to you.

Pastor: You, Lord, have promised not to tempt us beyond what we can endure; you, Lord, have shown us how to avoid temptation; and you, Lord, are ready to help us turn from the way of sin to the joy of righteousness.

All: Hear us when we call to you, O God.

Assistant: Voices assail us — those of friends, those of enemies, those of complete strangers. They question our faith; they belittle our values; they make us doubt our most treasured beliefs. From every side we are urged to give up on you, O God, and to embrace the ways of the world.

People: You, O God, have left your mark in every tree, in the grasses of the field, in the beauty of each flower, that we may be aware of your presence, your goodness, and your love for us.

Pastor: You, Lord, have shown your love for us in spite of our lapses into rebellion. Before we hear the voices tempting us, we know your voice of command, of invitation, of forgiveness, and of promise. May your voice block out all others, and be the one voice to which we listen.

All: Speak to us as we listen for your voice, O God.

Assistant: Many around us are not bothered by sin, even to denying that it exists. Many do not care about you, Lord, and feel no guilt at anything they do. We are tempted to follow their lead and excuse ourselves of wrongdoing.

People: You, O God, do not desire that we stagger under a heavy burden of guilt, and you take no delight in laying upon us restrictions and penalties; neither can you look away when your people rebel against you.

Pastor: You, Lord, have so clearly declared the futility of our attempts to rationalize our selfishness, and you have clearly shown us what is right and good. We cannot escape the reality that we do the things we know are wrong, and overlook the things we know are right. Our only hope is your forgiveness.

All: Pardon our sins for the sake of Jesus, O God.

Assistant: There is one source of sin: our rebellion against you, O God.

People: There is one source of salvation: your holy grace given us in Jesus Christ.

All: Move us to repent, and forgive us for your Son's sake, O Lord God, our Salvation.

(Other petitions may be included here.)

Pastor: All that we pray we offer in trust that you will hear us for the sake of Jesus, our Lord and Savior.

All: *Amen (Our Father . . .)*

Lent 2

Pastor: Almighty God, you called Abraham ages ago in order to begin a special people through whom you could bring blessing to all people.

Assistant: Now, in this time, you have called people into your church, that through them you can bring blessing to all in the world.

People: In baptism we have become your called and chosen people, Lord. Make us those who reflect, in our living, the great love you have for all whom you have made.

Pastor: In the call of Abraham, you asked him to leave his home and family to follow where you would lead him.

Assistant: Many of us are called within our families, and are sent to serve in our familiar workplace.

People: Lead us away from those people and those places which would prevent or interfere with our response to you, O God.

Pastor: In leading Abraham forth, you declared that you would show him the way to go.

Assistant: Many of us feel your guidance in our lives.

People: We pray that you may continue to go with us on our journey through life.

Pastor: As you showed Abraham the promised land which would be given to his descendants, he built an altar and worshiped you.

Assistant: In response to your call of us, we also come to worship you.

People: In our worship, may we acknowledge your greatness and your caring love.

Pastor: Father Abraham left all that was familiar and ventured toward a new home, because he trusted in you, Lord God.

Assistant: Work in us the same kind of trust, that we may follow your call throughout our lives.

People: We are your people through no merit of our own, but as those who live by faith in you, O Lord God Almighty!

(Other petitions may be included here.)

Pastor: Keep us in our faith by the power of your Holy Spirit, and bring us into your eternal presence through the loving gift of your Son, Jesus Christ;

All: Who with you and the Spirit is one God, now and forever. *Amen (Our Father . . .)*

Lent 3

Assistant: How easily we take for granted some of the basic blessings of our lives, O Lord.

People: We take for granted opening a faucet and getting water; we grumble and complain when it rains for more than a brief time.

Pastor: Open our eyes, Lord God, and give us an appreciation of the ordinary gifts you give us.

Assistant: How easily we take for granted the basic gift of your grace to us, O Lord.

People: In an offhand way we bow before you to confess our sins, and then we walk away thinking of them no more.

Pastor: Open our eyes, Lord God, and help us to appreciate the costly giving by which your Son died for us.

Assistant: How easily we take for granted our worship of you, O Lord.

People: We grumble and complain if what we do in worship is not to our liking, and allow many other interests to draw us away from worship.

Pastor: Open our eyes, Lord God, to the values of worship for us, and focus us, in our worship, on you, our God.

Assistant: How easily we take for granted our witness for you, O Lord.

People: We fail to speak of our faith. We forget the effects of our actions on others. We decline daily opportunities to invite others to consider your will and your love.

Pastor: Open our eyes to the many hurts and needs around us which could be helped by our speaking of our own faith and showing our own trust in you, O God.

Assistant: How easily we take for granted the friendship you make possible, O Lord.

People: We fear being your enemies, yet struggle in vain to make up for all that separates us from you.

Pastor: Open our eyes to the salvation you have given us, the peace that comes from faith and trust in the saving death of Jesus, the Christ.

(Other petitions may be included here.)

Assistant: Lord God, you are not to be taken for granted, but you are to be all in all for us.

People: Give us thankful hearts for your blessings; willing hearts in worship and service; open hearts as we witness your love; and peaceful hearts as we are confident in our being your redeemed people.

Pastor: And to you, O God, be all thanks and praise for your gracious goodness, which made us, and saves us, and gives us new and eternal life!

All: Amen (Our Father . . .)

Lent 4

Assistant: We all think we know what it is to see, Lord, even if we give no thought at all to the marvel of sight.

Pastor: Yet you, O God, have declared through your Son that, while the blind have been given sight, those who see are blind.

People: Help us to understand your meaning, O God, that true seeing is a gift from you to help us look beyond ourselves and to see you in the others who are around us.

Assistant: We all think we know what it is to know the truth, Lord, even if we tend to think that our truth is better than another's.

Pastor: Yet you, O God, have declared through your apostle that truth is revealed only in your light.

People: Help us to understand your truth, O God, that we may reject the worthless and hold on to that which counts.

Assistant: We all think that we know who the most worthy, valuable, and important people are, Lord, even as we are often willing to overlook many others whom we consider of no account.

Pastor: Yet you, O God, have declared, through your prophet, that you value persons not by how they look, but by what lies within them.

People: Help us to understand your evaluation of all persons, O God, realizing that you love us all, desire our good, and strive to bring all into your presence.

Assistant: On our own, all of us, in blindness, grope for the truth and fail to recognize the worth of ourselves and others.

Pastor: You, Lord God, would give us sight, enlighten us with truth, and put us into relationship with one another and with you.

People: Lead us from darkness into your wondrous light, O God, and anoint us with your Spirit, that we may have the power to live as those on whom the light of Christ shines.

(Other petitions may be included here.)

Pastor: To you we give our praise and thanks, for you are our Creator, Redeemer, and Sanctifier:

People: Father, Son, and Holy Spirit, One God forever. *Amen (Our Father . . .)*

Lent 5

Pastor: We celebrate this day the incredible patience which is yours, O God, as you work out your eternal plan of salvation for those whom you have made.

Assistant: You called a people to be your own,

People: That they might be those who would show faith in you, and bring blessing to all others.

Assistant: You blessed and punished those you called,

People: Giving them all they needed to prosper and thrive, and acting to keep them from being lost to you.

Assistant: You restored those who remained faithful, and continued to give them their heritage,

People: Raising up dry bones and causing them to live once more.

Pastor: Blessed are you, O God, for your gracious actions for your people. Praise to you, O God, for the love that will not let us go. Glory and honor to you, O God, for even to this day you have continued to restore to you those of faith.

All: Call us, and bless us; correct us, and restore us, O Lord God.

Pastor: We celebrate this day the inscrutable power by which you can bring even the dead to life, O God.

Assistant: Your holy people were all but blotted out, and you led them back to their land.

People: Thank you for preserving your people Israel, for from among them your promised Messiah came forth.

Assistant: Lazarus fell sick and died, and Jesus wept.

People: Thank you for giving Lazarus life again, to be a sign of the power of your presence with our Lord.

Assistant: Jesus died on the cross for us, and was laid in the grave.

People: Thank you for raising Jesus from the dead, that he could be the first one of those whom you will bring forth to be in your eternal kingdom.

Pastor: We are in awe of your power, O God, for you have created life and overcome chaos; you have defeated death and brought about the resurrection to new life.

All: Lead us, O God, through death, which ends life here; to resurrection, which brings us into your perfect presence.

(Other petitions may be included here.)

Pastor: As our Lord Jesus died for all nations, so renew in us strong and true faith, that trusting him, we may live and die and rise again by your almighty power.

All: Through Jesus Christ, your Son, our Lord. *Amen (Our Father . . .)*

Lent 6
Passion or Palm Sunday

(Based on a hymn text by Henry H. Milman)

Assistant: *Ride on, ride on in majesty!*
   Hear all the tribes hosanna cry.

Pastor: Peoples of many times and a multitude of nations have praised you, Lord Jesus Christ.

People: We praise you, and sing our hosannas to you, for you are the One who has the right to direct and guide our lives!

Assistant: *O Savior meek, your road pursue,*
   With palms and scattered garments strewed.

Pastor: Your humble life has inspired generation upon generation to respond to you in faith.

People: We acknowledge you, and the power of love by which you lived and through which you conquered death.

Assistant: *Ride on, ride on in majesty!*
   In lowly pomp ride on to die.

Pastor: In your death you have given the gift of life to all people, Lord Jesus.

People: You have given us life, for we trust in what you have done for us, and we draw strength and courage from your promise which sets us free from the fear that sin will destroy us.

Assistant: *Bow your meek head to mortal pain,*
   Then take, O Christ, your pow'r and reign!

Pastor: You gave us the most precious gift you could, and you bore the pain for all in your innocent death.

People: God has exalted you, your name is honored by all faithful people, and you are the Lord of Lords, the King of Kings, the One who is worthy to rule our lives and the lives of all people.

(Other petitions may be included here.)

Pastor: Go with us through this Holy Week, Lord Jesus, and, as we relive your suffering and death, strengthen in us the resolve to commit ourselves to you alone, that we may be saved from the power of sin and dwell with you eternally!

All: Amen (Our Father . . .)

A Prayer for Holy Week

Assistant: Let us pray to God, who through his Son has come to us to face the worst that we, in our rebellion, could do to him.

Pastor: Lord God, in our sin we again and again cause you suffering, rejection, and the separation of death.

People: In this Holy Week, we recall all that Jesus suffered at the hands of rebellious people; turn us from such sin, and help us to receive the Savior of all peoples into our hearts.

Assistant: Let us pray to God, who did not send angels to destroy people, but who, in the strength of love, lived out sin's worst assault.

Pastor: Lord God, in our sin we hurt you again with our apathy, our ignoring of your way, our fascination with the ways of the world.

People: In this Holy Week, help us to turn from all that offends you, and renew in us the love which responds to your gracious actions for us.

Assistant: Let us pray to God, who broke through the destruction of death to bring about the victory of resurrection.

Pastor: Lord God, no accomplishments of humans, no marvels of the created world, no combination of good qualities in the universe could do what you have done in overcoming death and proclaiming new life.

A Prayer for Holy Week

People: In this Holy Week, give us faith to trust in your resurrection, prepared for us; and empower us to be people who live in this hope.

Assistant: Let us pray to God, who stands with us in death and in life, who destroys and makes alive, who creates and re-creates.

Pastor: Lord God, all others pale before your presence. All others fail to measure up to you. All others lack that which you possess and give in fulness.

People: In this Holy Week, let us know your love for us more than anything else; for we see that love in the suffering, death, and resurrection of Jesus Christ our Lord.

All: All honor and praise and glory be to you, Father, Son, and Holy Spirit, now and forever! *Amen*

Maundy Thursday

Pastor: On this Holy Day, Lord Jesus, we rejoice in the gift you have given your people, hidden in the eating and drinking of the Eucharistic (Communion) meal, the food and drink of eternal life.

Assistant: You invite us to your meal, Lord Jesus.

People: May we come believing that you meet us here; and may we go with strength to trust and believe all that you have done for us.

Assistant: You feed us with the bread of heaven.

People: May we be nourished so that our lives show forth the wonder of your grace.

Assistant: You satisfy us as no other food can do.

People: May we find our place to be within your family, secure and confident of your promise to us, able to risk living in obedience to your challenge.

Pastor: On this Holy Day, Lord Jesus, we rejoice in the example you have set before your followers, revealed in the washing of your disciples' feet, an action of humility and servanthood.

Assistant: You invite us to think of each other in this way, Lord Jesus.

People: May we approach each other knowing that each one is a child of God, dearly loved by the Creator, deserving of caring and esteem.

Assistant: You ask us to treat each other in this way.

People: May we exercise respect for those around us, living with them as we would like them to live with us.

Assistant: You instruct us to teach others to follow your example.

People: May we tell our children of your way of servanthood, and prize qualities of serving in one another.

Pastor: On this Holy Day, Lord Jesus, we rejoice in the new commandment that you have set before your people, making love for others as we ourselves are loved the key to our life together.

Assistant: You proclaim the love of God for us, Lord Jesus.

People: May we allow that love into our lives, that we may feel good to know that our God cares for us.

Assistant: You show your love for us, especially in your obedience unto death.

People: May we sincerely trust all that you have done for us, Jesus, finding in your sacrifice the foundation on which we can build our lives.

Assistant: You encourage us to love others as we have been loved.

People: May we be known by our love, which we share in word and deed with all whom we know and meet.

(Other petitions may be included here.)

Pastor: On this Holy Day, Lord Jesus, we eat and drink in communion with you and all your people; we learn to be servants in your name; and we receive the gift of love, that we may share it again.

All: Glory and praise to you, O Lord, now and forever. *Amen (Our Father . . .)*

Good Friday

Assistant: Hear us as we pray to you, Lord God, on this awe-ful day that you made good.

Pastor: While the power of sin was doing its worst, marshaling the hatred and fear of ordinary people, and the jealousy and greed of political and religious leaders:

People: You, O God, were working for good, taking on the sins of all, using the strength of love to defeat the power of evil.

Pastor: Overcome in us the grip which evil has on us;

People: And instill in us the power of love, helping us to live renewed lives.

Assistant: Hear us as we pray to you for our world, Lord God, which in these troubled times reflects only dimly your good creation.

Pastor: While sin is abroad in the world, invading the peoples of all nations, and concentrating its force in actions of violence and destruction:

People: You, O God, continue to call to righteousness any who will heed your invitation, any who seek the way of peace and good will.

Pastor: Act in the lives of your faithful people;

People: And make your church in every place an active influence for good.

Assistant: Hear us as we pray to you for the days which lie ahead, both good and bad.

Pastor: While we continue in this life, we are caught in the struggle of good with evil, of creation with destruction, of life with death.

People: You, O God, become our only hope that good, and creation, and life will be victorious.

Pastor: Help us to look to Jesus, who died on the cross for us and for all people;

People: And send us your Holy Spirit, to forgive, to call to faith, to work in us the fruits of godly living.

Assistant: Hear our prayers this Good Friday.

Pastor: Strengthen us in our baptism into your Son's death;

People: And bring us to the present renewal and final victory of eternal life.

All: Through Jesus Christ, your Son, our Lord, who lives and reigns with you and the Holy Spirit, one God now and forever. *Amen*

Easter

Assistant: We have been called together by the good news of resurrection: of death defeated, of sin overcome.

People: Hear us, God, as we lift our voices in prayer: that sin may be overcome in our lives, death defeated for us, and resurrection raise us to your presence.

Pastor: Through your apostle, you have called us to look to you, and not to get lost in the world, which has gone astray from its creator.

People: Help us to set our hearts on you, Lord Jesus, the risen Savior, that depending on you alone, we will share your glory.

Pastor: Through the leader of the disciples, you have enlightened us with the truth: that death cannot hold those who are yours.

People: Fulfill your promise to us, Lord Jesus, and fill us with new life from God.

Pastor: Through the resurrection of Jesus, you brought about the completion of your new covenant of life.

People: Make us present-day witnesses to your power of love, and help us always to live in the joy of your victory.

Assistant: We are sent forth to carry the good news of resurrection, of life, and of forgiveness into every place we will be.

People: Hear us, O God, as we seek your enabling power to live out these gifts in our world.

Pastor: Through your Son, you have done everything needed to set us free.

People: Help us to bring freedom to our relationships, as we repent and forgive, that we may be at peace with one another.

Pastor: Through your disciple, you have shown us the power of speaking the truth.

People: Give us the willingness to speak, in the power of love, to those who fear and doubt and despair, that they may find your truth.

Pastor: Through your apostle, you have pointed us to the new life in Christ.

People: Empower us by your Spirit to live out the life of love which we have been shown, and which leads to eternal life with you.

(Other petitions may be included here.)

Assistant: We, your people, are called and sent in the name of the Lord Jesus Christ, who was dead but now lives; whom we now know by faith, but will see when he comes in glory.

People: All praise and honor and glory to you, O God, for your victory in Jesus Christ, our risen Lord and Savior! *Amen (Our Father . . .)*

Easter 2

Pastor: Lord Jesus, we your disciples of today look upon your first disciples with both envy and compassion; help us to learn from them.

Assistant: The twelve were with you and saw your mighty acts and heard your gracious words.

People: We often wish we could have been among them, and indeed give thanks that they told what they saw and heard, so others might come to faith.

Assistant: Though locked in hiding, ten wonder-filled followers beheld your risen glory, and heard your word of peace.

People: We can only imagine their joy and the awe which struck them dumb; and, we are grateful for their witness to your appearing.

Assistant: At times, like Thomas, we cannot bring ourselves to believe what we have not personally experienced.

People: We ask for your understanding, and pray that we may acknowledge you our Lord and God.

Pastor: Lord Jesus, we your people of today know that we cannot expect to follow you without encountering trials and testing; help us to endure until life eternal.

Assistant: We have the living hope which the resurrection of Jesus Christ brings to all who believe.

People: We live in that hope by your power and with your assistance, for you stand with us in every circumstance of life.

Assistant: We look forward to the rich blessings you prepare for us in your holy kingdom, and even now we glimpse the goodness you make ready for us.

People: We are richly blessed and gifted, and pray for your help to use all we have received for good.

Assistant: We know suffering, and our faith is tested in the arena of this world, where evil strives to draw us from you, and seeks to destroy our every hope.

People: We seek to endure the testing, Lord, and know that you are by our side to help us continue in our love for you, whom we have not yet seen face to face.

Pastor: Lord Jesus, you died for us, and for our salvation God raised you from the dead, that sin and death would no more have dominion over us. Help us live as those who are your own.

Assistant: And hearing your good news, may we receive the gifts of grace in Baptism and Holy Communion;

People: We who in this day are disciples and followers and people of Jesus of Nazareth, God's Son, our Savior!

(Other petitions may be included here.)

Pastor: (Concluding the other petitions.) *Amen (Our Father . . .)*

Easter 3

Assistant: We long for your people to live in close fellowship with one another, Lord God.

Pastor: But first, we need to turn away from sinful jealousies and misunderstandings, and unite in our commitment to Jesus, the Christ.

People: Bring us together through the gift of your forgiveness, and renew the power of the Holy Spirit among us.

Pastor: We hear again your promise to call us to yourself.

People: Turn us to you, Lord, and hold us in true faith, that we may know your salvation.

Assistant: We long to know the meaning of your work from of old, Lord God.

Pastor: Through prophets and other faithful writers, you have shared your will in the Holy Scriptures.

People: Direct us to the writings which show your plan to save your people.

Pastor: As we learn from the Bible, help us to respond to your Word with lives of faith.

People: Strengthen us to live by your guidance, and to be obedient to your will.

Assistant: We long to stand before the judge of all, as those set free, Lord God.

Pastor: Your judgments are fair, and your regard for each one is the same as for all.

People: Mercifully regard us, O God, and see all that Christ has done to save us.

Pastor: You have bought us with the priceless gift of our Savior's obedient death.

People: May our hope and trust in you be lived out in reverence and in confident gratitude.

(Other petitions may be included here.)

Assistant: As we have beheld the glory of the risen Savior, so may we be your witnesses in every way, inviting others to faith in you, and holding to our beliefs until that day you come to receive us into your presence.

People: Victory is yours, O God, through Jesus Christ, your Son, our Lord. *Amen (Our Father . . .)*

Easter 4

Assistant: Lord Jesus, you are the one who leads us to the kingdom of God.

Pastor: We ask for the courage to follow you, that we may enter the kingdom as chosen and welcomed children of the Lord.

Assistant: Lord Jesus, your voice is the one which calls us to kingdom living.

Pastor: We need to listen to your truth, for indeed there is no other which can guide us to the living God.

People: We ask for the strength to be committed to your way, that we may actually be your people here and in the time to come.

Assistant: Lord Jesus, your life, death, and resurrection are the genuine pathway to eternal life.

Pastor: We cannot repeat the life you lived, for indeed you are the one and only Savior by whom God has redeemed all people.

People: We ask for the grace your life bestows, that we may be judged not in terms of our own merit, but in the light of your saving help.

Assistant: Lord Jesus, our following you may take us through the pain of undeserved suffering.

Pastor: We will be tempted to turn aside, because there are many easier paths.

People: We ask you to guard us against the wiles of the Evil One, that we may not give in to that which will destroy us.

Assistant: Lord Jesus, you have shown us the power of love to overcome evil.

Pastor: We need to recall your sinlessness, your quiet patience, your hope in God; because these won a victory which lies and accusations and force could not gain.

People: We ask you to help us die to sin, that we may live for righteousness.

Assistant: Lord Jesus, you have come to give us life in all its fulness.

Pastor: We need the gift of your life, for indeed none other can make us alive.

People: We ask for the life you alone give, that we may be alive now and forever.

(Other petitions may be included here.)

Pastor: Good Shepherd of all, bestow on us the gracious gifts of our loving God, and lead us into peace.

All: You are the Savior, Redeemer, and Mediator for all who trust in you, Lord Jesus Christ! *Amen (Our Father . . .)*

Easter 5

Pastor: Lord God Almighty, we people of your creation reject again and again the very One through whom you would make us your people of faith.

Assistant: In seeking for power, wealth, honor, and fame,

People: We disregard your love for us, as shown in the life of Jesus of Nazareth.

Assistant: Our strife, our distrust, our jealousies, our hatreds,

People: All are evidences that we have not learned from Jesus.

Assistant: The suffering which sin causes — the hunger, poverty, sickness, and murder —

People: All are evidences that we have not listened to your guidance for our lives.

Pastor: Holy Lord, you continue to turn upside down the values of peoples everywhere, and you show us that the One rejected is still the way, the truth, and the life.

Assistant: our temples are still built

People: From the living stones of believing peoples who have been won to faith by the Lord Jesus.

Assistant: The cornerstone of true life in this realm is still revealed;

People:　　The very Lord who suffered and died for us, whom you raised to eternal glory.

Assistant:　From all nations and peoples, you choose your own holy nation:

People:　　The church of Jesus Christ, which witnesses your love, speaks your word, experiences your mercy.

Pastor:　　Merciful God, lead your people from anxiety and fearful worrying to confident faith and trust in you through your Son.

Assistant:　Though we know of Jesus, we at times fail to see in him your gracious presence.

People:　　Let us hear your Word, receive your grace, feel your presence, and thus be those who believe in you.

Assistant:　Today and every day, we live in the strength of having Jesus as our Lord and Savior;

People:　　For he is the One who has gone ahead of us to prepare a place in the presence of God.

Assistant:　Today and every day, we are ready to have life here end for us,

People:　　Knowing that you are coming again to receive us into the kingdom of God.

(Other petitions may be included here.)

Pastor:　　Forgive us, renew us, refresh us, and save us, Lord God, for the sake of him who died for all;

All:　　Even Jesus Christ our Lord, who lives and reigns with you and the Holy Spirit, now and forever. *Amen (Our Father . . .)*

Easter 6

Assistant: We have placed the symbols of our gods in every nation, in every city, in every house, and in every life.

Pastor: In your sight, O God, that which we value most — our god — is truly known.

People: You do not regard the pretense of our words, or simply our outward actions, but you know the values we hold in our innermost beings.

Pastor: Many times we struggle to place you above all else, Lord God.

People: Just as many times we fail in our ability to keep you first in our lives.

Pastor: You have clearly declared you will not share our loyalties with that which is less than your holiness.

People: We throw ourselves on your mercy, O God, asking your forgiveness for our disobedience, and seeking your gracious help to honor you as we should.

Assistant; There is one symbol which you would place in us, that by which we might live here and now, and for all eternity.

Pastor: As you are Love, O God, so you seek to place love in us.

People: For if we love you, Lord, we will respond to you with obedience and loyalty and trust.

Pastor: In Baptism you have granted us your love.

People: From the beginning of our relationship with you, love has been your way of dealing with us, and love has been the response you desire.

Pastor: Even more, you give us the Holy Spirit, who seeks to work in us the way of love.

People: Be our helper, Holy Spirit, that we may never be alone or without the precious power of love.

Assistant: Even as we struggle to have you as the One God of our lives, you ask us to be witnesses to our hope.

Pastor: May we be willing to tell others of our ongoing endeavor to honor you as the one, true God.

People: In our witness, help us to listen and understand the problems and needs of others.

Pastor: May we try our best to do good, even if it leads to derision by others.

People: Defend us from giving in to evil, and when we do, grant us your forgiveness.

Pastor: As those forgiven, strengthen us to forgive others.

People: And by our forgiveness in your name, reach those who live in darkness, that they may see new light and life.

(Other petitions may be included here.)

Assistant: Lord God, you never abandon us to aloneness, even when we turn from you and despair in our self-imposed solitary confinement.

Pastor: Be with us, O God, and stay with us always,

People: That love may be at the center of our beings, and love may show itself to all we meet.

All: In Jesus' name. *Amen (Our Father . . .)*

Ascension Day

Assistant: Lord Jesus Christ, you came into our realm, giving up your equality with God, so you could bring us to peace with our Creator.

Pastor: With signs and wonders and gracious words, you proclaimed a new day for all God's people.

People: Because of your coming among us, we know the peace of forgiveness, the joy of relationship with God.

Pastor: With your obedient death on the cross, you have taken away our sins and granted us new life.

People: As we follow you, we find the way of rightness, that God may be seen and glorified.

Assistant: When you had accomplished all that the Lord gave you to do, you left your disciples, so the Spirit might come to bring them the power of new life.

Pastor: By your command, your people have become your witnesses.

People: Live in and through us, Lord Jesus, for we answer your call to be your followers.

Pastor: Call us, enlighten us, empower us to be the people of God.

People: Work in us all that will show forth your presence in this world.

Assistant: Lord Jesus, you are now in glory in the presence of the Lord Almighty, and we have you as our advocate before the Maker of the universe.

Pastor: Though we do not see you now, Jesus, we welcome your presence with us in Word and Sacrament.

People: Enlighten us and feed us, that we may have the means of grace within us.

Pastor: We believe that you will come again, and in glory bring together all believers into the mighty presence of God.

People: Keep us for that day — in faith, in righteousness, and in hope.

(Other petitions may be included here.)

Pastor: Lord Jesus, by your wondrous birth, your gracious life, your suffering and death, your glorious resurrection, and your mighty ascension, we are made your people.

People: Keep us in your church, now and ever, and bring us at last into the kingdom eternal. *Amen (Our Father . . .)*

Easter 7

Pastor: Lord God, at the call of your Spirit we have been together at worship this day, seeking the knowledge and strength to go and live the days ahead.

Assistant: We cannot stay here, absorbed in prayer and praise;

People: Yet help us to pray at all times, and to make our lives a praise of you, O God.

Assistant: By your Word and Sacrament, nourish us to live as your people.

People: Help us to hear your guidance always, and to receive your presence wherever we may be.

Pastor: Lord God, life springs its surprises on us, testing us painfully, trying us sharply.

Assistant: Without your help we cannot withstand the testing;

People: But we trust you to be with us, and to help us through to confident faith.

Assistant: In every trial we look to you for help,

People: And rely on you to show us the way through.

Pastor: Lord God, our confidence is in your having chosen us, redeemed us, given us your Son.

People: We believe that you have given us to Jesus, that his church will continue in this, our time.

Assistant: Now keep us your own,

People: That we may be one with you, as you and your Son are one.

(Other petitions may be included here.)

Pastor: You promise to send your Spirit to us, O God.

People: May we receive the Spirit with ready hearts, and live in the truth to which he ever leads us.

All: We pray in the name of our Lord, Jesus Christ. *Amen (Our Father . . .)*

The Day of Pentecost

Assistant: Come Holy Spirit, be the one who leads us to all truth.

Pastor: Truth evades us, and we are confused by the many claims and counter-claims of the voices we hear.

People: You bring to light the truth of Jesus, the Christ, and you lead us to walk in this truth as followers of the Son of God.

Assistant: Come Holy Spirit, be the one who calms our fears.

Pastor: Fears assail us, and we are in terror of events and peoples; uncertainty and strife surround us.

People: You bring us the reality of confident hope, and instill in us the love of Jesus, which drives out all fear.

Assistant: Come Holy Spirit, be the one who grants us vision.

Pastor: We are insecure in facing the future, and want only to hang on to what we have known.

People: You bring us the wonder of that which is yet to be, and empower us to strive on toward that which our God would have us do in his name.

Assistant: Come Holy Spirit, be the one who unites us in faith.

Pastor: Disbelief, doubt, and bizarre religious beliefs confront us and confuse us.

People: You bring us the clear proclamation of salvation in Jesus Christ, and work in us faith that this salvation is ours by God's grace.

Assistant: Come Holy Spirit, be the one who gives us joy.

Pastor: Gloom and despair are common in our world, for people often see only hatred and strife, and our best efforts cannot overcome them.

People: You bring us the good news that God has acted in Christ to defeat the powers of darkness, overcoming sin and death for us, that we may rejoice.

Assistant: Come Holy Spirit, be the one who keeps us for eternity.

Pastor: All things are passing away, and judgment will divide the righteous and unrighteous for all eternity.

People: You bring us the love of Jesus, which covers our sin and brings us into life eternal, that we may live forever in the presence of our God.

(Other petitions may be included here.)

Assistant: Come Holy Spirit, be the one who goes with us into life.

Pastor: Day by day we make decisions, carry out plans, relate to others, respond to you.

People: You bring us the abundant life of the Creator, the saving love of the Son, and your own sanctifying power. Come, Holy Spirit!

All: *Amen. (Our Father . . .)*

The Holy Trinity

Pastor: This day, Lord God, we recall all your mighty acts, all that you have done for your people of every time and place.

Assistant: By your creation, all things were made, and you called them good.

People: Give us a true appreciation for your creation, Lord, that we may care for all you have given us, as you command.

Assistant: By your call and with your mighty power, you gathered a people and cared for them, leading them from death to life.

People: We praise you for Abraham and Sarah, persons of faith; for Moses and Miriam, leaders of the Exodus; for all who have been your people and have fulfilled your promise.

Pastor: Today, Lord God, we set ourselves among those who have been redeemed and restored by the life, death, and resurrection of Jesus, the Christ.

Assistant: In coming among us, Jesus was able to show your love and your will more clearly than any other revelation.

People: Jesus has made us your friends, O God, and we rejoice in his saving life.

Assistant: By the call of Jesus, we are commissioned to teach all nations your gracious will.

People: In message proclaimed and in deeds lived out, enable us to be your witnesses in this time and place.

Assistant: As Jesus has died for us, and in him you have given us victory over sin and death, so make us ambassadors of his love.

People: Receive in baptism all who are graciously presented before you, Lord, and hold us to you in promise for all eternity.

Pastor: Now, Lord God, we commit ourselves to live by the power of the Spirit, that we may be forgiven, and risk lives of loving service.

Assistant: In our fellowship in your church, nurture us and strengthen us with the Word and Sacraments.

People: May we live in the covenant of our Baptism, and feed on the gifts of Holy Communion, even as we hear and obey your Word.

Assistant: Bring forth from us the fruits of love and joy, peace and hope, right living and merciful service.

People: In word and deed, make us the reflection of your love to others, off-setting the destruction and evil of those who reject you.

Assistant: Revive your people when they are downcast, and renew in us the zeal for you that accomplishes wonders.

People: Make of us the miracle of your might, O God, that your presence in the world may be revealed.

(Other petitions may be included here.)

Pastor: We ask for your love, O God, that we may be filled with it.

Assistant: We ask for your grace, Lord Jesus, that we may abide in it.

People: We ask for your fellowship, Holy Spirit, that in it we may truly live.

All: All glory and honor to you, Father, Son, and Holy Spirit, one God now and forever! *Amen (Our Father . . .)*

Proper 4 — *May 29-June 4* (Common)
Pentecost 2 (Lutheran)

Pastor: We have called on you again and again, Lord God, for you have invited us to come to you in prayer, putting into thoughts and words our needs, our desires, and our concerns.

Assistant: But even now you make us aware that we can pray just words, with no thoughts behind them, no trust that they are heard, no awareness that you already know all our needs.

People: Help us never to pray "Lord, Lord!" in meaningless repetition, but faithfully to call upon your name in sincere and heartfelt prayer.

Pastor: We have spoken your Word again and again, Lord God, for you have commanded us to go forth and teach all people, that they may have the opportunity to become part of your eternal kingdom.

Assistant: But even now you make us aware that we can speak our own word, and not yours; that we can try to use you to accomplish our own ends of achieving fame and honor; that we can pronounce your Word while we neglect doing it ourselves.

People: Help us that we never carelessly toss your Word to and fro, in order to gain something for ourselves, but lovingly share what we know to be true, that others may find you, believe in you, and follow you.

Pastor: We have done all kinds of things to please you, Lord God; keeping commandments, doing rituals, observing customs and days, even separating ourselves from those we despise.

Proper 4 — May 29-June 4 (Common)
Pentecost 2 (Lutheran)

Assistant: But even now you make us aware that we can do nothing to save ourselves, and that our sin surely separates us from you.

People: Help us never to depend on ourselves, but always to turn in trust to you, who through our Lord Jesus Christ has put us right with you, giving us the peace of life in your forgiveness and grace.

(Other petitions may be included here.)

Pastor: Now, Lord God, move in our lives to make us your own.

Assistant: Establish us on the strong foundation of faith in Jesus Christ.

People: Help us always to live in the security of relationship with our Savior, Lord, and Friend, Jesus Christ, in whose name we pray. *Amen (Our Father . . .)*

Proper 5 — *June 5-11* *(Common)*
Pentecost 3 *(Lutheran)*

Pastor:	Lord God, all around us in our world are people that we are sure will never come to faith in you.
Assistant:	They don't attend church; they don't read the Bible. They don't steer clear of the ways of the world.
People:	Therefore, we don't invite them to worship, or seek their friendship, or have much hope for their eternal destiny.
Pastor:	Then we read of Jesus, and think about his way of reaching to the most unlikely persons to be his followers.
Assistant:	For example, a tax collector, one of the most hated functionaries of the day. This is who Jesus stopped to invite to be his disciple!
People:	The thought that you love all people, and the recognition that some of your followers were unlikely surprises leads us to re-examine our conclusions, our fears, and our timidity in asking all we meet to respond to you.
Pastor:	Open our eyes and our ears, Lord, that we may not be blinded by labels and quick impressions of others.
Assistant:	Give us the kind of insight which is yours, and which we observed in Jesus as he walked among us.
People:	Let us look beyond outward religious activity in people, and watch for the words and actions of kindness which reveal those who are touched by your Spirit.

Proper 5 — *June 5-11* *(Common)*
Pentecost 3 *(Lutheran)*

Pastor: Even more, Lord God, call us away from any false dependence on religious practice.

Assistant: Help us to know our need for being saved.

People: Impress upon our hearts your call to live out our faith by reflecting your love and by obeying your will for us to care for one another.

(Other petitions may be included here.)

Pastor: As we trust in you above all else, free us to serve in your name.

People: That peoples of all kinds, dispositions, temperaments, and attitudes may be drawn to your love and your kingdom. *Amen (Our Father . . .)*

Proper 6 — *June 12-18* *(Common)*
Pentecost 4 *(Lutheran)*

Pastor: Lord Jesus, your ministry set the tone for the ministry of the church, even for this, our day.

Assistant: You took your message of Good News to the people.

People: You travel to us, Lord; you speak so we can understand, and you touch the needs and hurts we have, Lord.

Assistant: You announced the coming of the Kingdom of God.

People: We long for your reign in our lives, so we can know God's love for us, so we can feel our worth, so we have the strength to live for one another.

Assistant: You brought healing to those who were sick.

People: Our ills are many, in spite of miracles of medicine; and, our need for your touch, which can make us whole, is overwhelming.

Pastor: Lord Jesus, in this time there are crowds without a leader; we run to and fro with no direction. In spite of all our God-given potential, we are still to be pitied.

Assistant: You continue to challenge your church with a harvest larger than we can imagine.

People: We continue to agonize over the lack of laborers for the harvest.

Assistant: You continue to invite us to prayerful trust in the Lord of the harvest.

Proper 6 — *June 12-18* (Common)
Pentecost 4 (Lutheran)

People: We continue to complain about the lack of laborers for the harvest.

Assistant: You continue to hope for the rescue of the lost, the turning of the strayed, the enlightenment of those who have not heard.

People: We continue to despair over the lack of laborers for the harvest.

Pastor: Lord Jesus, call your people together, and bestow on us the power to witness to your great love for all those whom you have made.

Assistant: Work through us to drive away evil.

People: Help us to be clear about your will, your commandments, and your direction for living.

Assistant: Work through us to heal sickness.

People: Help us to know our value and worth so that wellness becomes a goal for ourselves and others.

Assistant: Work through us to overcome death.

People: Help us witness our hope in eternal life, and accept life's endings as new beginnings.

(Other petitions may be included here.)

Pastor: On our own, each of us is turned away from you.

Assistant: By your call we are disciples, persons learning from you.

People: By your grace we are witnesses to you, that faith may spring forth, and a chosen people may glorify you.

All: Lord Jesus, send us forth to call the world's people to you! *Amen (Our Father . . .)*

Proper 7 *June 19-25* *(Common)*
Pentecost 5 *(Lutheran)*

Assistant: Sin is a reality of our life, Lord God: it lies at the heart of so many of our woes; it plagues us with struggles in which we so often find ourselves helpless.

Pastor: The rebellion of one person has spread to all of us, and death is the result which sin produces.

People: In your mercy, save us from the sin of individuals, which leads to the hurt and destruction of many lives.

Pastor: The law shows us the right; but we are incapable of keeping the law, and it only angers and frustrates us.

People: In your mercy, print your law upon us, so that we do not excuse ourselves into damnation, but turn to you for help.

Assistant: We are followers of Christ, and you have made it clear, Lord God, that we cannot expect to be liked or treated better than he was.

Pastor: What do we have to fear, Lord, when we see the glory to which Christ was raised?

People: Help us boldly tell forth your Word, persistently invite to faith, and convincingly live out our discipleship.

Pastor: How can we avoid following Jesus, when to do so is to lose our own place in your kingdom?

Proper 7 — *June 19-25* *(Common)*
Pentecost 5 *(Lutheran)*

People: We cannot be perfect, Lord, but we can be faithful in trusting you and speaking your name in love.

Assistant: From of old, your people have declared their trust in you, for you rescued them from evil, you showed them you were on their side.

Pastor: Evil is around us and within us.

People: Save us and rescue us, O God, and allow us to live in your forgiveness.

Pastor: Draw us to your side,

People: Making us unafraid to speak for you, to teach your way, to show your love.

Pastor: Bring us to your kingdom,

People: Along with all those whom you redeem through Christ our Lord.

(Other petitions may be included here.)

Assistant: Glorify yourself through your people, the church;

People: And rule your world in love and peace, now and forever.

All: *Amen (Our Father . . .)*

Proper 8 — *June 26-July 2* *(Common)*
Pentecost 6 *(Lutheran)*

Pastor: Lord Jesus, we often characterize you as a lovely, meek, person who is non-threatening to all; but you have shown us that your coming brought division, enmity, and violence.

Assistant: There is struggle within as we try to determine where our primary loyalty will be.

People: By nature we are turned in on self; we prize our own desires. We strive to be self-sufficient; and although we fail, we do not easily turn to you for help.

Assistant: Others claim our loyalty and try to control us, as we exert influence where we can.

People: The love of marriage is tainted with jealousy. The joy of children is tarnished with possessiveness. The kinship of community is blemished with prejudice.

Pastor: You, Lord Jesus, would enrich our every relationship as we accept you as our Lord, place you first in our living, and respect you more than any other.

Assistant: You willingly gave up equality with God to be one of us.

People: Help us to give up doing everything our own way so we can be one with you.

Assistant: You willingly suffered death on the cross to end the power of death and evil, as you arose victorious.

People: Help us to take up our cross to follow you, knowing that as we suffer death with you, so we will rise to eternal life with you.

Proper 8 — *June 26-July 2* (Common)
Pentecost 6 (Lutheran)

Pastor: Lord Jesus, your strength is seen in your standing firm in your trust of God, unswayed by the enticements and power-plays of this world.

Assistant: Over and over again, we have tried in every way imaginable to gain life, extend life, preserve life.

People: Every attempt fails, and our lot is still to die.

Assistant: We see in you, and in those who follow you, actual peace in the face of death, a willingness to be true to God in spite of death.

People: And we are witnesses to your resurrection and to the power of lives given up in service to your holy name.

Pastor: Lord Jesus, empower us, as we trust in you, to stand firm in our faith in you, that we may know your love which never lets us go!

(Other petitions may be included here.)

Assistant: We pray in the name of Jesus Christ, our Lord and Savior,

People: Who is one with you, O God, and with the Holy Spirit, now and eternally. *Amen (Our Father . . .)*

Proper 9 — *July 3-9* *(Common)*
Pentecost 7 *(Lutheran)*

[Based on Matthew 11:28-30 TEV]

Assistant: Jesus said: "Come to me, all of you who are tired from carrying heavy loads."

People: How often we feel weighed down with burdens and cares, struggles and frustrations, hurts and hatreds.

Pastor: Jesus, our Savior, we turn to you as you have invited; we bring to you our loads and lay them at your feet, recognizing in you the one who can help us — the person of God who stands with us in the experiences of life.

People: We thank you for your invitation, and we come to you, Lord Jesus.

Assistant: Jesus said, "Take my yoke and put it on you."

People: How often we feel confined in the yokes of peer pressure, of corporate practice, of societal expectations, of angers and defeats.

Pastor: Jesus, our Master, we pray to receive your yoke, that we may find ourselves striving to live with you at our side, recognizing your strength to move us purposefully through our journey in this world.

People: We thank you for your yoke, an identification with you, Lord Jesus.

Assistant: Jesus said: "Learn from me, because I am gentle and humble in spirit."

People: How often gentleness is absent from our lives, and humbleness is regarded as weakness.

Pastor: Jesus, our Companion, we welcome your gentleness which manifests itself in concern and care for those whom God has made; we seek your humility which showed itself in your complete confidence in who you are, so that you did not have to praise yourself or lord your power over others.

Proper 9 — July 3-9 (Common)
Pentecost 7 (Lutheran)

People: We thank you for caring for us, and live in the confidence of being yours.

Assistant: Jesus said: "I will give you rest; you will find rest."

People: How often we are aware that although we sleep every night, and although we have much leisure time, we seldom find rest: our minds worry on, our bodies are tense, our spirits are down-cast.

Pastor: Jesus, our Redeemer, we beseech you to give us rest which will refresh our minds and bodies and revitalize our spirits, that we may live with a sense of purpose and confidence and worth.

People: We thank you for the tranquility available to your people as they experience your presence with them and come to depend on you.

Assistant: Jesus said: "The yoke I will give you is easy, and the load I will put on you is light."

People: How often we have run from your yoke and complained of your load.

Pastor: Jesus, our Lord, rule in our lives so we will not have to struggle alone; so we will have tasks of true worth to carry out; so we can hope for everlasting life with you.

People: We thank you for all you give us, all you do for us, and for our chance to stand with you.

(Other petitions may be included here.)

Assistant: Hear our prayers for the sake of Jesus Christ, our Lord.

All: *Amen (Our Father . . .)*

Proper 10 — *July 10-16* *(Common)*
Pentecost 8 *(Lutheran)*

Pastor: Almighty God, we find great beauty and wonder in the world you have created; yet you have revealed to us that all we see and know will not compare to the glory you will one day reveal to those who stand in your holy presence.

Assistant: Likewise, we are puzzled and offended by the suffering we endure and which we see in the lives of those around us; yet you have declared, through your apostle, that when your glory is revealed, we will recall suffering no more.

People: Lord God, give us a sense of awe as we view your creation. Give us trust and confidence in your power and presence as we endure suffering. But most of all, hold us unto you, that we may come into your glory forever.

Pastor: Almighty God, we know from the experiences of living that every good effort is thwarted by the forces of apathy, confusion, and outright evil; but we also know that your good finds receptive lives in which to establish itself in order to bring forth resounding results.

Assistant: Likewise, we understand the differences which we, as people, present to you: some with childlike trust, others with smug disdain, yet others confused and uncertain, and some in outright rebellion against you.

Proper 10 — *July 10-15* *(Common)*
Pentecost 8 *(Lutheran)*

People: Lord God, we are amazed at the generosity of your working, speaking your Word to all, that although rejected or ignored in some lives, it may be heard and treasured and responded to in others; open our ears to hear you and our hearts and wills to respond to you.

(Other petitions may be included here.)

Pastor: We live in confident trust that the word you speak is not wasted, is not sent forth in futility.

Assistant: We believe that your Word accomplishes what it says, and brings forth faith, trust, and righteousness.

People: We hear your Word, O God, and it changes our lives: speak to us that we may live and be changed for eternal life with you.

All: Through Jesus Christ, our Lord. *Amen (Our Father . . .)*

Proper 11 — *July 17-23* (Common)
Pentecost 9 (Lutheran)

Assistant: How are we to understand the frustration of life, O God: that evil is forever trying to attack and destroy good?

People: Our own efforts at good are thwarted, and the positive influences of persons in society are wrecked again and again.

Pastor: Creator of the Universe, you have made us so we can know you and love you: may this suffice until we live with you in your eternal kingdom.

Assistant: In this life, faithful people exist side by side with those who disregard your very being, O God.

People: In zealous fervor, we at times seek to eliminate those we consider unworthy of your blessings.

Pastor: Ruler of all beings, you have called us not as judges of others, but as faithful witnesses to your love; transform our world as we speak and show your loving power to all.

Assistant: History seems to prove hopeless our quest to bring about a better world in which to live.

People: Every human effort seems riddled with problems, and even the good life we enjoy is plagued with anxieties and guilts.

Pastor: Lord of all time, give us patience to live in this time between the times, side by side with your enemies, but always with hope that the day of our Lord will come, and on that day you will surely fulfill your promise to us and make us your glorious kingdom.

Proper 11 — *July 17-23* (Common)
Pentecost 9 (Lutheran)

(Other petitions may be included here.)

Pastor: As we mark our days in this life, give us your Spirit, that we may hear your Word and know your will.

People: By the Spirit, help us to pray and trust, for you hear us and help us.

All: For the sake of Jesus Christ, your Son, our Lord. *Amen (Our Father . . .)*

Proper 12 — *July 24-30* *(Common)*
Pentecost 10 *(Lutheran)*

Pastor: Lord God, you have again and again asked us to pray to you, promising to hear our prayers and responding to us according to your love for us in Jesus Christ.

Assistant: Your servant, Solomon, recognized his need for your help to rule your people, and he asked for the gift of wisdom.

People: In our several situations in life, give us that which we most need, O God: a lively and saving faith in all you have done for us in Jesus Christ!

Pastor: Not only do you hear our prayers, O God, but it is your desire and will to work good in the lives of those who love you.

Assistant: In spite of all he suffered and endured, your servant, Paul, trusted in your goodness and boldly witnessed your gracious works.

People: Day after day be with us, O God, and work your good for us.

Pastor: Our confidence comes not from our understanding of your being, nor from our place among your people, but from the plan to save us which you have revealed.

Assistant: You have chosen us to be your people, and you have called us to faith through the Gospel of your Son.

Proper 12 — *July 24-30* *(Common)*
Pentecost 10 *(Lutheran)*

People: On our own we would be separated from you; you have made us right with yourself through our Lord Jesus Christ, and our hope is in your bringing us to stand in your glory.

Pastor: Let us never become apathetic about your kingdom, Lord, but always regard it as the most precious thing we could find or seek.

Assistant: All people are of your creation, and every one is valuable to you; but you declare that those who turn from you will therefore choose not to be part of your kingdom, and will have no place with you for eternity.

People: Even as we bring some understanding to our response to you, O God, we are still in need of the new wisdom which you alone can give us. Grant us faithfulness to trust you always.

(Other petitions may be included here.)

Pastor: We offer these our prayers as you have commanded us,

People: In the name of Jesus Christ, your Son, our Savior. *Amen (Our Father . . .)*

Proper 13 — *July 31-August 6* *(Common)*
Pentecost 11 *(Lutheran)*

Assistant: Death is our worst and final enemy, O God.

People: We try to ignore it, cover it up, ridicule it, overcome it, but death is still with us. We feel its tug time after time; we see it around us, and it strikes terror in our hearts.

Pastor: Lord Jesus, you recognized the power of death to intimidate the lives of God's people; you were saddened by the death of your cousin, John.

People: Help us, Lord Jesus, when we feel the pain of the death of those we love.

Assistant: Your apostle declares that the power of death is fear.

People: So we set our minds to living, we busy ourselves with others in relationships of caring and love, and we strive to make a difference in our world as we pass this way only once. But when we are idle, or reflective, or shaken up, there is death, ready to separate us from everything we value and hold dear.

Pastor: Your apostle Paul struggled to answer this concern for those to whom he taught the Gospel, and he named the many things that could possibly separate us from the love of Christ.

People: Speak to our inmost hearts, O God, and give us faith that nothing in the whole creation can cause that separation for us!

Assistant: Death has been overcome by life, O God, giver of life.

Proper 13 — *July 31-August 6* (Common)
Pentecost 11 (Lutheran)

People: We can live with confidence, Lord, through our faith that we are victors through Christ; and we can answer your invitation to come and gain what is really worth having: a covenant with you that will last forever.

Pastor: God, you are with us as the one who sees our plight and takes pity on us; as the one who heals our sinful ills; as the one who feeds us the bread of life; as the one who spreads an eternal banquet feast for us.

People: If you will never let us go, we can endure the death which ends life here and begins life in your heavenly kingdom — for those we love and for ourselves. Hear our prayer to hold us to you in life and in death!

(Other petitions may be included here.)

Assistant: Hear our prayers, eternal Lord, and save us for the sake of Jesus Christ,

People: Who lives and reigns with you and the Holy Spirit, one God, now and forever. *Amen (Our Father . . .)*

Proper 14 — *August 7-13* *(Common)*
Pentecost 12 *(Lutheran)*

Assistant: In this time of prayer, let us be aware of all who feel a sense of hopelessness and despair.

Pastor: We name before you, O God; the poor, the homeless, those whose system of government gives them no rights, the unemployed, the grieving, the battered, the persecuted, and others whom we name in our hearts.

People: You met Elijah long ago in his despair, and spoke to him in the still, small voice which followed the wind and earthquake and fire; so be with those who see no hope in this day through the small voice spoken and lived through your people, the church.

Assistant: As we are in prayer, let us be aware of all who have turned away from God and no longer know the comfort of his love.

Pastor: We name before you, O God; the persons disappointed by the church, the persons embittered by sickness or sorrow, the persons too busy to bother with you, the persons overwhelmed with the diversions afforded by our times, the persons who have decided you do not exist, and others whom we name in our hearts.

People: As Paul expressed sorrow and pain that his own people turned from your gracious love in Jesus, so we beseech your forgiveness for any we have turned from you, and ask you to use every means to bring the Gospel to those who do not know it.

Proper 14 — *August 7-13* (Common)
Pentecost 12 *(Lutheran)*

Assistant: As we offer our prayers to God, let us be aware of all who are in danger of slipping from God's kingdom of love.

Pastor: We name before you, O God: those in the agony of terminal illness or nearing death in some other way, those who are tempted to deny you, those whose trust in you is wavering, and others whom we name in our hearts.

People: Peter sought to walk to you on the water, then faltered in his trust, and sank into the waves, calling on you for help; so we pray you to hear the cries of all who call to you, and implore you to help save them.

Assistant: Along with our prayers for others, let us be aware of our own despair, turning aside, and danger of slipping from you.

Pastor: We name before you, O God: the times we have lacked trust, the times we have been angry, the times we have tired of obedience, the times we have felt hatred, the times we have wanted that which would destroy us, and other times which we name in our hearts.

People: Elijah, Paul, and Peter answered your call and continued in their lives of faith, showing bold confidence in you, O God; so help us that we may continue in our beliefs and in our response to you, certain of our salvation, through Jesus Christ our Lord.

(Other petitions may be included here.)

Pastor: We thank you for hearing these our prayers,

People: For the sake of Jesus Christ. *Amen (Our Father . . .)*

Proper 15 — *August 14-20* *(Common)*
Pentecost 13 *(Lutheran)*

Assistant: All these years and centuries after you walked among us, we find ourselves in a world where more people *do not* know and believe in you than do, Lord Jesus.

People: How are we to think of ourselves and others in this situation; how can we be your people, Lord Jesus?

Pastor: Long ago, the Prophet spoke to the people, telling them to do what is right and just. All people need justice, no matter what their beliefs, their station in life, their nationality, or their religion or lack of religion.

People: Help us to live with respect for others, striving to support justice for all.

Assistant: Your message of love could not be contained among the chosen people, but soon burst forth as others responded to the good news of your death and resurrection.

People: How are we to react when those who did not grow up in churches or belong to families of faith turn to you, Lord Jesus?

Pastor: In your own ministry, there were those who heard of your Godly power and sought you out. Your gifts are needed by the people of our time as well.

People: Extend your gracious blessing to all in need, Lord Jesus.

Assistant: Today, as long ago, people get locked into their attitudes and beliefs, often rejecting you.

Proper 15 — *August 14-20* (Common)
Pentecost 13 (Lutheran)

People: How are we to be channels of your grace to others, and not blocks which prevent people from knowing you, Lord Jesus?

Pastor: Paul hoped great things for his kinsfolk who could not bring themselves to respond to your actions for them. His hope was in the mercy God has for those lost in disobedience.

People: Give us hope for all people, and permit us to approach all people with the invitation to come to you.

(Other petitions may be included here.)

Pastor: Save us and all people, Lord Jesus,

People: For you are the Savior of all, who lives and reigns with the Father and the Holy Spirit, one God, now and always. *Amen (Our Father . . .)*

Proper 16 — *August 21-27* (Common)
Pentecost 14(Lutheran)

Pastor: We worship you, Christ our Savior. We learn of your life and work; we trust in all you have done for us. But we, too, have difficulty answering the question of who others say that you are.

Assistant: Some name you the essence of sweetness and tenderness; some regard you as the one who will fulfill our wishes; some call on you in anger or in excitement.

People: The variety of answers and opinions about you is puzzling and troublesome, and we ask your help not to be confused by what many say.

Pastor: In our worship and learning and living, we find you challenging us to declare who we believe you to be.

Assistant: As we name you our Lord, as we call you our Savior, and as we regard you the Prince of Peace, we know there is one relationship we cannot miss:

People: You are the Son of God, the Messiah, the Christ, the one who comes in the name of the Lord God Almighty!

Pastor: Help us to see that we do not make up who you are, Lord Jesus Christ; but open our eyes to the help of the Spirit, who calls forth from us true faith.

Assistant: There is none who knows you well enough to describe you; no one has knowledge of you by which to have control over you.

People: We can declare your relationship with God only because it is revealed to us.

Proper 16 — *August 21-27* *(Common)*
Pentecost 14 *(Lutheran)*

Pastor: Upon the faith of Peter and the disciples, you founded your church, and established its faith in the
knowledge of the Savior.

Assistant: Continue that faith in us and in all those who are
your church, that no other idea, ideology, or ideal
will displace the clear trust we have in you, Jesus.

People: Keep us in this faith, and help us to declare it to
those who join us in your holy church, that you may
continue to work your salvation in this and coming
generations.

(Other petitions may be included here.)

Pastor: You have made us, and all that there is.

People: To you, Lord Jesus Christ, be all glory, as you live
and reign with the Father and the Holy Spirit, one
God, now and forever. *Amen (Our Father . . .)*

Proper 17 — *August 28-September 3* *(Common)*
Pentecost 15 *(Lutheran)*

Pastor: Almighty God, although we are your creation, made for relationship with you and provided with guidance to live as you intend, we are drawn into following the patterns of living in this world.

Assistant: In separation from you, we bend truth, corrupt righteousness, ignore mercy, and pervert justice.

People: Call us again to be transformed, to be made new by your power within us.

Pastor: Jesus, our Lord, you came into our world and here you experienced all of the temptations of greed, power, selfishness, and evil which try to divert us from your way.

Assistant: You clearly knew your mission, and showed the caring love of the Lord God in spite of opposition, apathy, and rejection.

People: You faced unjust condemnation and death rather than conform yourself to the world.

Pastor: O God, you have made us your people through the victory of Jesus, the Christ, over the power of evil, and you call us to follow our Lord.

Assistant: Our following presents us day by day with decisions and choices, even as you show us the path of true discipleship.

People: With the help of your Spirit, may we offer ourselves in living sacrifice and service to you, O God.

Proper 17 — *August 28-September 3* *(Common)*
Pentecost 15*(Lutheran)*

Pastor: Urged by the world to preserve ourselves, to live for self, to grab and keep life's blessings, we find ourselves losing relationship with you, God — in danger of separation from you for eternity.

Assistant: Inspired by Christ to give of ourselves, to live for others, to share God-given blessings, we find satisfying and joyful fellowship with you and with one another.

People: So may we respond to you and discover the joy of life in your name.

(Other petitions may be included here.)

Pastor: Help us to live as your people, a single body with many parts which make up the whole.

Assistant: Help each of us to use what you have given us so your body, the church, may be strong and vital.

People: Help us to accept our part among your people with modesty, yet with willingness to serve you as you give us strength.

All: Bring us to your kingdom, through the merits of Jesus Christ, your Son, our Lord. *Amen (Our Father . . .)*

Proper 18 — *September 4-10* *(Common)*
Pentecost 16 *(Lutheran)*

Assistant: Our relationship to authority is a major issue of our lives, O God, and this day we ask your guidance and help to discern our relationships with those over, around, and under us in our society.

Pastor: At various times, we find ourselves under parents, teachers, employers, leaders, governmental authorities, and your sovereign rule.

People: Give us respect for those who are in authority over us, and bless us with wise and just leadership for our lives.

Pastor: We live among others, many of whom share the values of honesty, responsibility, and regard for the rights of others; but some of whom are given to devising their own rules for living, which violate the freedom of those around them.

People: Call us to lives of justice and righteousness, O God, and provide the means to correct and limit the behavior of those who disrespect others.

Pastor: The weight of authority at times rests upon us, and amid all of the ambiguities of living, we are called upon to guide, correct, discipline, and judge.

People: Help us to be responsible and caring in the exercise of power over others, always conscious of the source of our authority in you, and the results of our actions on those in our care.

Assistant: You, O God, have shown us through your Son the way to be reconciled to another, and through your apostle you have revealed the wisdom of living within the just rule of official authority.

Proper 18 — *September 4-10* (Common)
Pentecost 16 (Lutheran)

Pastor: Your way of settling disagreement and dispute is one which allows mutual respect and caring, engaging the resources of the fellowship of believers.

People: Help us to confront broken relationships in a way which permits healing, forgiveness, and renewal.

Pastor: Your wisdom that those who do good need not fear authorities gives us a way to order our lives, and provides a test for discerning evil authority.

People: Help us to live in society without fear, but call us to challenge any who rule by showing favor to the evil or by persecuting the innocent.

Pastor: Most of all, you point us beyond laws, rules, and judgments, as you give us the commandment to love our neighbor as ourself.

People: Help us to live by love, that we may thus fulfill the whole law, and discover the best relationship of all — that which we have with you.

(Other petitions may be included here.)

Assistant: Order our lives in your peace, O God,

People: That we may live in harmony with those around us all our days.

All: Amen (Our Father . . .)

Proper 19 — *September 11-17* *(Common)*
Pentecost 17 *(Lutheran)*

Pastor: You, O God, have shown us that forgiveness is as necessary for our lives as the air we breathe and the food we eat.

Assistant: Help us to accept your forgiveness, available to all who turn toward you,

People: That we may live in your forgiveness, no longer carrying and dragging the burdens which our sin heaps upon us.

Assistant: Help us to be forgiving, reconciling ourselves to one another in love,

People: That we may live with each other in harmony and peace, ending strife and conflict.

Pastor: You, O God, have taught us that forgiveness is not to be carefully counted out, with a meticulous eye on some limit.

Assistant: Help us to grasp the generosity of your forgiving, which begins and goes on far beyond our expectation,

People: That we may realaze we are loved so much we can turn to you with any problem, sin, or burden.

Assistant: Help us to resolve the enmity between ourselves and others with a forgiving spirit which removes anger and misunderstanding,

People: That we may restore relationships and rise to new levels of cooperation and mutual support.

Proper 19 — *September 11-17* *(Common)*
Pentecost 17*(Lutheran)*

Pastor: You, O God, have declared that we cannot play the game of forgive and remember, nor make a pretense of pardon while still harboring a grudge in our heart.

Assistant: Help us to do more than gloss over injustice, malice, and evil,

People: That we may not simply swallow our hurt, only to have it eat away at us, or surface in unexpected and inappropriate ways.

Assistant: Help us to confront the problems between ourselves and others with caring, honesty, and the sincere desire to bring about accord,

People: That we and they may find the possibility of deeper and more satisfying relationships.

(Other petitions may be included here.)

Pastor: Thank you for your gift of forgiveness,

Assistant: Which gives us peace with you

People: And peace with one another.

All: *Amen (Our Father . . .)*

Proper 20 — *September 18-24* *(Common)*
Pentecost 18 *(Lutheran)*

Pastor: Lord God, again and again we are struck by your graciousness, which goes so far beyond fairness and ordinary justice, that we constantly find our usual values turned upside down.

Assistant: We praise you for regarding each of us through your love, not judging us by comparing us with others.

People: Grant us a proper sense of awe at your mighty love, which rewards everyone with the same gift of eternal life.

Assistant: We seek your help, that we not become careless about response to you, thinking we can turn to you at a later time.

People: Give us the joy of a lifelong walk in your presence; or the satisfaction of turning to you in the time of vital maturity; or the encouragement of completing life in your favor.

Pastor: Almighty God, we are torn between living for you, and coming to the end of this life that we may be with you forever.

Assistant: We contemplate the glory and fulfillment it will be to dwell in your perfect presence, out of the grasp of sin and evil, in the company of all who have loved you.

People: Endow us with faith and hope which will keep us in relationship with you now, that we may know your presence eternally.

Proper 20 — *September 18-24* *(Common)*
Pentecost 18 *(Lutheran)*

Assistant: We acknowledge your will for our present lives, that you may work your grace through us as we reach out to others in your name.

People: Entrust to us the special tasks for which you have called us as your people, and empower us to fulfill them.

(Other petitions may be included here.)

Pastor: Give us patience to await the time you have set for us to complete this life;

Assistant: And help us to anticipate our dwelling with you then by serving you now,

People: Even as we trust in our Lord Jesus Christ, and draw strength for living and dying from your Holy Spirit.

All: We pray to you, O God, in the name of the Lord Jesus, by the power of the Spirit. *Amen (Our Father . . .)*

Proper 21 — September 25-October 1 (Common)
Pentecost 19 (Lutheran)

Assistant: How easily we can rebel against you, Lord God.

Pastor: We too quickly blurt out our ridicule of your ways for us,

People: And then find ourselves failing at our own ways of living.

Pastor: We set ourselves up as knowing better than you,

People: And then find out that our knowledge does not help us.

Pastor: We push ourselves into the center of our worlds,

People: And then find the world will not revolve around us.

Assistant: How simply we could return to your grace and favor, Lord God.

Pastor: No matter what we have said against you, we can turn and do your will,

People: And find the joy and satisfaction of living in harmony with our Creator.

Pastor: We can gain real knowledge, the wisdom that respects your guidance,

People: And find that it serves us well as we make our way through this life.

Pastor: We can accept you into the first and foremost place of our lives,

People: And find that all else fits into its proper place as well.

Assistant: How easily we can be misguided in the way we respond to you, Lord God.

Proper 21 — *September 25-October 1* *(Common)*
Pentecost 19 *(Lutheran)*

Pastor: We attempt to organize our religion to apply to every conceivable situation;

People: And then we find that life is surprising, and you are surprising in the ways you meet us.

Pastor: We try to restrict you to narrow confines, so that much of our life is not affected by you;

People: And then you demonstrate to us that you are the Lord of all things.

Pastor: We consider you to be anything that we want you to be;

People: And then find that you are very specific in your revelation of yourself.

Assistant: How clearly we can come to regard you as you would have us know you, Lord God.

Pastor: We can explore your Holy Word for a multitude of examples of your will,

People: And apply what we learn to our own circumstances.

Pastor: We can draw upon the encouragement and fellowship of others who honor you,

People: And grow and develop in our appreciation of all you mean to us.

Pastor: We can be open to the working of your Holy Spirit,

People: And discover more power than we will ever need to live as your people.

(Other petitions may be included here.)

Assistant: Thank you for being our Lord and God,

People: And for making us your chosen and redeemed people!

All: *Amen (Our Father . . .)*

Proper 22 — *October 2-8* *(Common)*
Pentecost 20 *(Lutheran)*

Assistant: What dangers we risk when we are unfaithful to you, O God.

Pastor: You have given us everything we have and all that we are, and you ask only that we give you thanks, and honor you as Lord.

People: But we get to thinking that your gift is our possesion.

Pastor: You seek our obedience and cooperation in sharing what we have received — both our wealth and our faith — with others.

People: But we reason that if we reject you, we won't have to share anything.

Assistant: To convince us of your loving purpose, you came among us in the person of Jesus of Nazareth.

Pastor: His life of revealing your gracious will to forgive, to heal, to bless, and to save was shared with all.

People: But then and now, there are those who reject his life, for he does not live up to our expectations of your working.

Pastor: His death, although unjustified and cruel, is the very means by which you make possible our renewed relationship with you.

People: But by our disregard for Jesus we seek once more to dethrone you and put ourselves in your place.

Proper 22 — *October 2-8* (Common)
Pentecost 20 (Lutheran)

Assistant: Turn us around, Lord God, as we discover the meaning of the Scripture: "The stone which the builders rejected as worthless turned out to be the most important of all."

Pastor: Of all the things we can do or say, none affects us as immediately and as ultimately as our faithful, committed response to the call of Jesus Christ: "Follow me."

People: We pray that we may hear that call; we pray that we may make a positive response.

Pastor: Let us never risk the loss of our place in your kingdom, Lord.

People: With your help, let us be those who produce the proper fruits of faith.

(Other petitions may be included here.)

Pastor: Hear us for the sake of Jesus Christ, our Lord.

People: Amen (Our Father . . .)

Proper 23 — *October 9-15* *(Common)*
Pentecost 21 *(Lutheran)*

Pastor: Lord God, we often consider your way to be hard and unpleasant, difficult to understand and tough to carry out.

Assistant: Let us pray for all those who are taking it easy as a principle of life.

People: We pray, Lord, that this will not be an excuse, now or ever, that would separate us from your promised kingdom.

Pastor: Lord God, life offers us so many choices and options, and our world urges us to experience them all.

Assistant: Let us pray for all those who have other things to do, which prevent them from embracing faith in God.

People: We pray, Lord, that this will not be an excuse, now or ever, that would separate us from your promised kingdom.

Pastor: Lord God, you once condemned humans to labor for their food, but we have found in our work a means to success, and wealth, and accomplishment.

Assistant: Let us pray for all those who have time for little else than to work.

People: We pray, Lord, that this will not be an excuse, now or ever, that would seperate us from your promised kingdom.

Proper 23 — *October 9-15* (Common)
Pentecost 21 (Lutheran)

Pastor: Lord God, we find your ministers boring, your evangelists insulting, your committed people overzealous, your humble servants expendable.

Assistant: Let us pray for all those who are too sophisticated to hear God's call and invitation.

People: We pray, Lord, that this will not be an excuse, now or ever, that would separate us from your promised kingdom.

Pastor: Even now your great feast is prepared for all who accept your invitation and seek entrance to your kingdom by your gracious gift of Jesus, the Christ.

Assistant: Let us pray for every sinner who repents, for every faithful child who is committed to God, for every willing servant of Christ, for every chosen one of God.

People: We pray, Lord, that we may be counted among those who accept your invitation to be in the kingdom of eternal life.

(Other petitions may be included here.)

Pastor: Hear our prayers and hold us unto you

People: Now and forever. *Amen (Our Father . . .)*

130

Pastor: Lord God Almighty, protect us from the evil temptation to test you with insinuations and reservations, even as we honestly seek your help in understanding the dilemmas of life in our times.

Assistant: We are very aware of the sacred and the secular, Lord.

People: Help us not to separate them so much that we consider you confined to only part of life.

Assistant: We look to government to care for many of our society's needs.

People: Help us not overlook the people who need caring, concern, and love shown to them.

Assistant: We wonder about the way you work: we wonder if you are really a God of power and of love.

People: Help us not to become arrogant in our expectations of your performance, but instead to be humble in our acknowledgment of your wisdom.

Pastor: Eternal God, unite us in spirit with the first Christians, who received the Good News of your actions in Christ Jesus with lived-out faith, with hardworking love, and with unshakable hope.

Assistant: We remember how they stood up to misunderstanding, to ridicule, and to cruel persecution.

People: Give us living faith with which to overcome apathy, criticism, and rejection, O Lord.

Proper 24 — October 15-22 (Common)
Pentecost 22 (Lutheran)

Assistant: We remember how they shared all things with one another.

People: Give us vital love which begins with words and goes on to actions of caring and love.

Assistant: We remember how they went even to their deaths, firm in the hope of redemption through Christ the Savior.

People: Give us steadfast hope which will see us through all of the trials of life, and bring us at last into your glory.

(Other petitions may be included here.)

Pastor: Hear us, O Lord, for the sake of him who died for us,

People: Even Jesus Christ, your Son, our Lord.

All: *Amen (Our Father . . .)*

Proper 25 — *October 23-29* *(Common)*
Pentecost 23 *(Lutheran)*

Pastor: Gracious God, your great commandment reveals to us the first and central place you should have in our lives. Help us to comprehend that rather than restricting us, this command gives us a way to view life which frees us to be who we are meant to be.

Assistant: Help us to love you with our whole heart, O God.

People: May we be sincere in our faith and trust, that they will endure through good times and bad.

Assistant: Help us to love you with our whole soul, O God.

People: May we commit all of ourselves to you, that no part of our life or being would separate us from our relationship with you.

Assistant: Help us to love you with our whole mind, O God.

People: May we believe in you without reservation, that the reasoning of a world in rebellion against you may not destroy us.

Pastor: Loving God, your second commandment reveals to us the kind of regard we should have for others, and for self. Help us to perceive that, instead of unworkable foolishness, this command gives us an effective way to live at peace with one another.

Assistant:
Help us to love others.

People: May we care for those around us as we are cared for by you, Lord.

Proper 25 — October 23-29 (Common)
Pentecost 23 (Lutheran)

Assistant: Help us to love ourselves.

People: May we discern that your love gives us marvelous worth, and your gifts to us bestow on us untold value.

Assistant: Help us to love other persons as we love ourselves.

People: May we live by your wisdom of treating others as we ourselves want to be treated, and so trust your way of love fully.

(Other petitions may be included here.)

Pastor: The way of love is a way of openness to you and to others, O God.

Assistant: Help us to risk the way of love,

People: And thus to find the joy of being loved!

All: Through Jesus Christ, your Son, our Lord. *Amen (Our Father . . .)*

Reformation Sunday *(Lutheran)*

Pastor: Almighty Creator of the Universe, you had pity on your creatures who confused the things of creation with their maker, and who considered the many parts of creation gods.

Assistant: So you called Abram and Sari to begin a chosen people to whom you could reveal yourself as the one and only God.

People: Continue to call us away from anything we would regard as a god, and hold us to the worship of you only.

Pastor: Gracious Savior, Jesus Christ, in the fullness of time you came to free your people from the confines of the law.

Assistant: Your liberating actions have drawn people of every race and clan to faith.

People: Continue to free us from religious bargaining as we accept your loving actions for us.

Pastor: Guiding Holy Spirit, with signs and wonders you founded the church, a people who believe and live the Gospel.

Assistant: In spite of divisions and corruptions, by working renewal and by cleansing, you have made the church a laboratory of faith, hope, and love.

People: Continue to guide your church, that people everywhere may come to know you.

Reformation Sunday *(Lutheran)*

Pastor: Creator, Redeemer, and Sanctifier — one God — we pray you to work new wonders for and through those you call in faith.

Assistant: Bring about increasing understanding and unity for those who love you, coupled with insights into your mercy and truth.

People: Continue to help us grow toward the oneness you have planned for those who dwell in your holy presence.

(Other petitions may be included here.)

Pastor: Lord God, create in us new hearts;

Assistant: Lord Jesus, focus our faith in you;

People: Holy Spirit, strengthen us to live as your people.

All: All praise and honor and glory to you, O God. *Amen (Our Father . . .)*

All Saints Sunday

Assistant: In the midst of life, we are in death, O Lord our God!

People: Who, but you, O Lord, can help us and give us hope?

Pastor: We praise you this day, as we remember all who have lived, all who have died, all who are now in your loving care.

Assistant: With sorrow we are parted from those we have loved, and in time we will be taken from among those who love us.

People: You alone, O Lord, can give purpose and meaning to life and death.

Pastor: We beseech you this day, to give us such a sense of your presence that we may feel oneness with all who have trusted you.

Assistant: You have declared, and we believe, that a day is coming in which you will bring to fulfillment all that you have promised to your people.

People: In that day, all things and every person will be made new, and our mortal nature will take on immortality.

Pastor: We pray that we may continue in our faith so we shall hear the trumpet call and awaken in your likeness.

Assistant: So on this day we remember all your saints, those made holy by the power of the Spirit, through Christ the Savior.

People: We especially recall and entrust to you all those of
our fellowship, family, and acquaintance whom we
now name ~~in our hearts~~. (The names of persons ~~may~~ who
~~be read.~~) have died in the past year are read.
A single chime tolls after each name.)

Pastor: Receive each of your chosen ones, O God, and give
them perfect peace, holding them within your eternal love.

(Other petitions may be included ~~here~~.)

Assistant: We pray in the name of Jesus Christ our Lord,

People: Who has gone into death before us, that death will
no longer hold us who are destined for eternal life.

All: *Amen (Our Father . . .)*

Proper 26 — *October 30-November 5* (Common)
Pentecost 26 (Lutheran)

Pastor: We live in a time of revolution, O Lord, and we ourselves are those who honor the revolutionary beginning of our nation. Yet we also are governed by leaders for whom we did not vote, and officials about whom we have misgivings.

Assistant: We seek your help in being able to live with integrity when we do not agree with decisions and choices of our officials;

People: Help us to respect and obey those with proper authority over us.

Assistant: We ask your strength for resisting what is wrong in our government and among persons in power;

People: Help us to work with others to correct and renew our society.

Pastor: Those in authority have often shown themselves vulnerable to corruption and evil, rejecting your mandate, O God, that they rule justly and by right principles.

Assistant: We seek your help in being able to stand up to such misuse of authority.

People: Help us to bring about reform and correction in ways that call our officials to accountability.

Pastor: It is a great temptation for leaders to seek special favor, recognition, gifts, and benefits, in spite of your guidance that true leaders serve and help those over whom they have authority.

Proper 26 — *October 30-November 5* (Common)
Pentecost 26 (Lutheran)

Assistant: We pray to you to provide us leaders and officials who will have the interests of those they rule at heart.

People: As we remember that the men and women in government are just like ourselves, prevent us from according them undue flattery and praise.

(Other petitions may be included here.)

Pastor: You alone, O God, deserve our praise and honor and adulation.

Assistant: You alone are Teacher and Father for us, your people.

People: Help us to humble ourselves that we may be great with you.

All: Amen (Our Father . . .)

Proper 27 — *November 6-12* (Common)
Pentecost 24 (Lutheran)

Assistant: Lord God, the passing of so many centuries since you came among us in Jesus Christ has resulted in some strange ideas concerning the special day when history will end and all things will be made new.

Pastor: There are those who propose to have figured out your plan, announcing the time of your acting, or the design which will lead to your holy day.

People: Help us to anticipate your time of fulfilling the promises you have made, but make us wary of naming the day, which is known to you alone.

Pastor: There are those who, because of the passing of so much time, do not concern themselves with your day of reckoning, and imagine a future without ending.

People: Do not allow us to be lulled into apathy concerning your warnings, nor to give up on your promises.

Assistant: Lord God, there are many voices calling to us concerning the way in which we should be prepared for Christ to come again and usher in your eternal kingdom; similarly, there are those who urge us to put such foolishness out of mind.

Pastor: There are those who exhort utopian living; those who stress a personal decision; those who devise a particular philosophy; and all declare that only in their way can we be saved.

Proper 27 — November 6-12 (Common)
Pentecost 24 (Lutheran)

People: Help us to know that only by trusting your grace, given us in the life, death, and resurrection of Jesus Christ, can we be at peace concerning your holy day.

Pastor: There are those who teach, by word and action, that life is only here and now: schemes of all kinds entice us to live as if there is nothing beyond the moment.

People: Protect us from an attitude toward life which rejects you and your loving plan for us.

Assistant: Amid all of the tensions and satisfactions of living, how shall we prepare to receive you, Lord, and how can we be ready at the time of your acting?

Pastor: Guide us by your Spirit to walk with you now, growing in our love for you, expanding our service in your name, deepening our trust and hope for what you will do for us.

People: Keep us always ready by a daily life of prayer, praise, and thanksgiving, so that when you meet us in your new day, we may receive you with joy and gladness.

(Other petitions may be included here.)

Assistant: Hold us to you by faith.

Pastor: Busy our lives in service.

People: Mark all we do with love.

All: For the sake of Jesus Christ, your Son, our Lord, who lives and reigns with you and the Holy Spirit, one God now and forever. *Amen (Our Father . . .)*

Proper 28 — *November 13-19* *(Common)*
Pentecost 25 *(Lutheran)*

Assistant: O God, what is the purpose of our lives?

People: Each of us is special in your sight; help us to fulfill the unique purpose for which you have created us.

Assistant: O God, what is the purpose of our living?

People: Each of us contributes something distinctive to the human experience in this realm; help us to make a contribution of worth through our living.

Assistant: O God, what is the purpose of our being part of your people, the church?

People: Each of us has been called by the Spirit to a life of faith, hope, and love; help us as Christians to be channels of your coming to our world and its peoples.

Pastor: Mighty God, you have created us in love and set us on a course of meaningful life: give us your gracious help, that we will use all you have granted us to fulfill the promise you have instilled in us.

Assistant: O God, what is to be the outcome of our lives?

People: Each of us lives our span of time, and then will be called home to you; help us to make the most of the time you allot us.

Assistant: O God, what is to be the impact of our living?

People: Each of us is in relationship with others, whose lives we influence and affect; help us to be a positive and salutary presence for all we meet.

Proper 28 — *November 13-19* *(Common)*
Pentecost 25 *(Lutheran)*

Assistant: O God, what is to be the reward of our following you?

People: Each of us is promised eternal life with you; help us to know that no more valuable prize could be awarded us.

Pastor: Saving Lord, you have given us far more than we deserve or earn and it is your will that your gifts grow in us to the point of our sharing your glory. Save us from rejecting your grace or from hiding your gifts; but strengthen us to give and use all your blessings, to your honor and praise.

(Other petitions may be included here.)

Assistant: As you have given us grace upon grace,

People: So may we faithfully use and share your gifts;

Pastor: That in the end, you will bless us even more

All: With life eternal, through Jesus Christ, our Lord. *Amen (Our Father . . .)*

Pentecost 27 *(Lutheran only)*

Assistant: We, your people of faith, have been called to carry forth the word which you have spoken, Lord God, until that day when you shall make all things new.

Pastor: Empower us to announce your word of love and your word of judgment in our churches, in our homes, in our nation, and in our world, O God;

People: That people may know your will and your graciousness, and, in their living, turn to honor and praise you with words and actions.

Assistant: We, your people of faith, have been set within the fellowship of the church, that we may be encouraged and strengthened in our response to you, Lord God.

Pastor: Help us to be united with all others who strive to do your will, and aid us as we grow in our love for you and for one another;

People: So may we be sanctified, that we may dwell in your holy and perfect presence in the age to come.

Assistant: We, your people of faith, Lord God, know that every evil and sin, all destruction and death, and any weakness and failure will utterly perish as your righteous kingdom is established.

Pastor: Guide us through the maze of false claims of salvation to the one true source of reconciliation with you — Jesus Christ.

People: Thus may we survive all of the false paths to your realm, and follow the way, the truth, and the life.

(Other petitions may be included here.)

Assistant: Prevent us from trusting in anything which is passing away;

Pastor: And keep our eyes fixed on you alone,

People: That we may never lose sight of you, our God and our Salvation.

All: *Amen (Our Father . . .)*

Christic the King

Assistant: Jesus, the Christ: you are the King of kings; you are the Lord of lords.

People: Come to us now, as we pray to you, and be the King of our hearts and minds, the Lord of our lives.

Assistant: You Lord Jesus, have gone before us, through the experience of death and into the glory of eternal life, as the resurrected Son of God!

People: Be with us now, we pray, that we may have hope in the face of death, and joy in the resurrection into your presence.

Assistant: Great Shepherd, reaching for the lost and protecting your own:

People: Search us out should we stray from you, and renew in us the faith and trust which will keep us your own.

Pastor: Jesus, in your life among us, you showed your willingness and ability to touch people with saving power. Speak your gracious word to us, and as we hear and respond, make and keep us part of your people of faith.

Assistant: Jesus, you are King of kings and Lord of lords.

People: From your realm of glory, send us your presence, that we may know the power of your love.

Assistant: Jesus, you have conquered death and live as resurrected victor over sin.

People: Put the power of evil on notice that you have overcome all the enemies of God, and that nothing can separate your faithful people from you.

Assistant: Jesus, you lead us from your throne on high, that we may find everlasting rest.

People: Guide us through all that separates us from one another and from you, that we may be one with you, the Creator, and the Spirit.

Christj the King

Pastor: Mighty Lord Jesus, as you have ascended to the presence of God, and share with God all power and glory, so we beseech you to intercede for us, that we may be redeemed from sin and, by your merit, receive the gracious forgiveness which makes us at one with God.

Assistant: Jesus, be our King of kings, and Lord of lords.

People: Many voices clamor for our loyalty; help us to hear and acknowledge your voice above all others.

Assistant: Jesus, you conquer sin and death for us, and promise us resurrection.

People: We acknowledge our need of you, for we are powerless against the evil one; save us and keep us your own forever.

Assistant: Jesus, you point us to the actions in this life which show our regard for you and which serve you in love.

People: As we are blessed by you, so grant that we may be blessings to all we meet, helping their needs, serving as your presence for them, showing mercy and love.

Pastor: Lord Jesus, help us always know that it is our living actions and words which serve and honor you rather than any rituals or customs. Give us your strength, that we may live out our beliefs, live by our morals, live up to our salvation, given us by your gracious actions for us.

(Other petitions may be included here.)

Assistant: We praise and glorify you, Jesus Christ our Lord.

People: You are worthy of all honor and might.

Pastor: Make and keep us yours, now and forever.

All: *Amen (Our Father . . .)*